"April Shprintz's book is t .... the heart, through her own st .... to be authentic, brave, and above all, generous to ourselves and others. I recommend her book to anyone who needs a dose of encouragement, hope, or inspiration—which means everyone!"

— Libby Gill
Leadership coach & consultant
Author of *The Hope-Driven Leader*

"This book is a magnificent road map for personal and professional success. Her story is told through an entertaining, encouraging, and heart-touching autobiography, so you'll come away not only believing, but also KNOWING that you can accomplish whatever you set your mind to."

— Bob Burg
Coauthor of national bestseller *The Go-Giver*

"The emotions in these poignant vignettes from April's inspiring life take you on a rollercoaster ride that will make you laugh and cry. I read these stories in one sitting because I simply could not put it down. These are the stories of someone who never sees herself as a victim and who finds a way to persevere no matter how much the odds have been stacked against her. This is a beautiful book that you won't read just once. April, put me down for a lifetime supply of Magic Blue Rocks. Absolutely brilliant!"

— Scott MacGregor
Founder & CEO of Something New LLC 6x winner of the American Business Awards for Innovation Founder of Talent Champions Council
3x author of the *Standing O!* series

"April Shprintz believes in YOU! She embodies a mindset of generosity and provides lessons through personal stories to uplift, motivate, and inspire YOU to achieve YOUR dreams! *Magic Blue Rocks* is exceptionally well written, and you will feel as though you are copilot to April on her journey!"

— Jill E. Johnson
Operations Sergeant Major, U.S. Army

"For our dreams to become real, we must first believe that they're possible. Are you dreaming of the life you really want—or just the one you think you're capable of achieving? You can do anything, that's April's message. It starts with believing. In a half dozen irresistible examples, this little book shows you how to begin."

— Michael Long
Coauthor of bestseller *The Molecule of More*

"I fell in love with those Magic Blue Rocks and loved seeing them evolve into different areas of April's life. The heart and tenacity she had as a small girl and on her amazing and successful journey started with believing in herself. Her words are words we all need to hear. Even a small nugget of belief in ourselves can move mountains, just like April did."

— Sarah Nuse
Co-owner & CEO of Tippi Toes Inc.
Bestselling author of *Destined for Greatness*
Shark Tank alum

MAGIC
BLUE
ROCKS

The Secret to Doing *Anything*

APRIL SHPRINTZ

Magnanimous Press
MagicBlueRocks.com

Paperback ISBN: 978-1-7362658-0-2
Ebook ISBN: 978-1-7362658-1-9
Hardcover ISBN: 978-1-7362658-2-6
Audiobook ISBN: 978-1-7362658-3-3

Cover Design by Eled Cernik
Interior Layout by Amit Dey

Publisher's Cataloging-In-Publication Data
(Prepared by The Donohue Group, Inc.)

Names: Shprintz, April, author. | Burg, Bob, writer of supplementary
    textual content.
Title: Magic blue rocks : the secret to doing anything / April Shprintz ;
    [foreword by Bob Burg].
Description: [Palm Beach Gardens, Florida] : Magnanimous Press, [2021]
Identifiers: ISBN 9781736265802 (paperback) | ISBN 9781736265826
    (hardcover) | ISBN 9781736265819 (ebook)
Subjects: LCSH: Self-actualization (Psychology)--Anecdotes. | Self-
confidence--Anecdotes. | Success in business--Psychological aspects--
Anecdotes. | Shprintz, April--Anecdotes. | LCGFT: Anecdotes.
Classification: LCC BF637.S4 S56 2021 (print) | LCC BF637.S4 (ebook) |
    DDC 158.1--dc23

To Kerry Daigle for inspiring me to share
my stories, and to Sue Harper for inspiring
me to do most everything else

CONTENTS

FOREWORD

There are people, good people, who have achieved massive success and who are to be greatly admired for having done so. They've found a way to bring immense value to the marketplace and have been richly rewarded for doing so. Kudos to them!

Yet as successful as they've been, they're not necessarily someone from whom you'd believe you could learn to do the same, at least not in a way that would provide you with the tools and confidence to do so. For example, they might have one or two skill sets or qualities they were able to tap into that the rest of us don't have. Or while they are able to "do a thing," they don't have the patience or ability to teach others.

Thus while we can admire them, we probably wouldn't seek them out as mentors.

Then there are those very special people like my dear friend April Shprintz. Not special because they have those one or two amazing qualities such as her—special because they show us how everything they've done that has brought them the magnificent success they have attained, we can do as well.

And not only do they show us...they show us with love, with heart, with generosity!

Their biggest thrill is when someone else succeeds. Their greatest victory is when they help someone else to understand and then successfully apply the principles they've utilized in their own success journey.

Through this book, you are going to meet such a person. April is indeed one of the most successful people I know. Yes financially, but not only that. She is also immensely successful in a way that only one who is loved by all who know her can be said to be successful.

Success didn't come easy for her. She was not born with what might be called the *privilege* of a stable upbringing. Quite the opposite, in fact. And certainly not in terms of money. Absolutely not that. And not in terms of opportunity...at least not one in any way handed to her. She had to figure that out for herself.

What she did have was a combination of intelligence, confidence belying her circumstances, and more than anything else—belief. Belief that she was meant to be something more than who she began life as, and more than she was told she was by those closest to her.

Go back for a moment to that word *belief.* That's the key.

In the following pages, be prepared to learn what it takes to believe in yourself...to believe that whatever you truly want to become, you can become. Let April help you see that in yourself. It's there, and she's just the person to help you see it.

She's magnificent…just like you!

I wish you stratospheric success.

Bob Burg, coauthor of *The Go-Giver*

P.S. If you have children, if you have grandchildren—please buy a copy of this book for them. You'll understand why once you've read it yourself.

A NOTE TO THE READER

Dear Rockstar,

Yes I realize you are the reader, but to me you're also a rockstar. Maybe you already know that deep down inside, but in case no one has outright said it to you just yet, I'm saying it now.

There is something special in each and every one of us. Yet somehow, many of us have doubts or have never even heard just how special we are. I want to give you the gift of knowing that no matter how big your dream, no matter how stacked against you the odds seem, anything and everything is possible for you.

This book is full of stories about overcoming odds and following dreams just based on belief. My life story started with the craziest odds-defying thing I've done to date: simply being born.

My mother didn't know she was pregnant with me until she was nearly five months along. She had an internal noncancerous tumor that was so large she already looked as if she *were* pregnant. She had already scheduled the surgery to have it removed. However, once that growth's roommate kicked, she rushed to the doctor and the jig was up—there was also a baby!

The doctor advised her to end the pregnancy immediately because he thought the situation was so dire. He predicted that I would die, she would die, we would both die, or in the best case scenario, I'd be born extremely brain damaged. Sheesh! What a start.

Lucky for me, my mom had belief in me and the importance of me getting to live. My mother stubbornly believed that her little boy was going to be just fine. (Hey, she got part of it right!)

That was the greatest gift my mom ever gave me: fighting for me and believing I should get a chance to be here, when absolutely everyone else feared for her life and encouraged her not to have me.

I'm excited to say I defied the odds and made a loud and dramatic entrance into the world, shocking everyone by being healthy, happy…and a girl! My mom told me this story when I was very young, and I became convinced that I was a miracle child put on this earth to defy the odds.

It is my greatest hope that sharing these stories with you will give you belief in yourself so you'll know that anything is possible.

April

Chapter One

MAGIC BLUE ROCKS

"Oh, you're poor," my six-year-old schoolmate Brad said without looking up from his coloring.

What?! I thought. *I am not poor! That's horrible. There is no way I am that.*

Brad and I had been asked to do a special project at recess. We were undoubtedly, in my mind, the smartest kids in class. But what had started out as a big honor quickly took a hard left into don't-cry-because-you'll-look-like-a-baby territory.

While we waited for Mrs. Caldwell to bring us crayons for our project, Brad mentioned my jeans were too short. He thought my mom should buy me new ones.

Some people might think that was weird for one six-year-old to say to another, but it made sense coming from Brad. He didn't think like me. He saw life more logically and paid attention to details I couldn't be bothered with—like how far my jeans went down my legs.

In my opinion, there were so many more important topics to think about, like how this project meant we were definitely special. However, I liked Brad, so I was happy to explain to him, "It doesn't matter that these jeans aren't long enough. Soon it'll be spring, and we'll cut them into shorts!"

Brad nodded. "Okay, that solves what to do with those jeans, but you still need new ones that are long enough."

I sighed. I felt like Brad should know how clothes shopping worked. He was the smartest kid I knew. Since he often explained subjects to me that were more "his area," I was happy to help him understand this concept from my perspective.

"You only buy new clothes once a year, when it's time for school to start. Same for shoes."

That's when he said it, just matter-of-factly, like he was answering a math problem instead of *changing my world* with one sentence.

"Oh, you're poor."

I looked at him like he had two heads as my mind revolted at the word.

"I am absolutely NOT poor," I stated, sitting up straighter and crossing my arms.

I could see Brad was thinking. I was too.

Mrs. Caldwell interrupted to give us our crayons and tell us to be good while she went to check on the kids at recess.

I barely heard her. My mind was reeling. There was no way I could be poor. The grass proved it!

We had moved to this tiny little town in Tennessee (that you couldn't find on a map) only a few months before. We'd left Cleveland, Ohio, where we lived in a basement apartment near what my mom called "the inner city."

We lived in an area where a lot of people were poor. My mom talked about people who were "less fortunate" than us a lot, so I didn't think we were like them. Logically, we must be *more* fortunate.

The biggest difference in the poor area of Cleveland and the nicer areas of the city was grass. There was no grass to be found in the poor area, unless a little had been planted around a tree on the edge of the sidewalk. Where the rich people lived in the big fancy houses, there was a lot of grass. They each had their own yard, and I figured out on my own that grass equaled rich.

While I didn't want to move to this new state called Tennessee and meet a bunch of relatives I didn't know, I changed my tune when I noticed our little house was surrounded by—you guessed it—grass. It was a big deal!

There was more grass than I'd seen at the prettiest houses in Cleveland. We were movin' on up.

I wasn't sure Brad would understand what grass meant, since he never lived in Cleveland, so I kept my argument simple. "I'm really not poor. I'm just not."

Brad tilted his head and squinted. "Okay, what does your dad do?"

That seemed like a weird question. I don't know why he was asking about someone I rarely saw.

"But my dad doesn't even live here. He lives in Ohio," I replied.

"What does your mom do?"

"She's a waitress."

Brad nodded and then asked one last question: "Do you get free lunch?"

The moment he asked, my bravado disappeared and my stomach fell. My mind was flooded with memories I hadn't paid a lot of attention to before that moment.

The weird-smelling building my mom took me to in Cleveland where they gave us huge packages of cheese and peanut butter for free (my friends didn't have those packages in their kitchens).

The nice people from church bringing us boxes of food week after week when we moved to Tennessee.

Days at home with my sister without power while Mom worked extra shifts to get the electricity turned back on.

I felt that awful prickling in my nose, the telltale sign I was going to cry. My eyes welled up with tears. The knots in my stomach tightened even more, and I knew crying about being poor made it even worse.

So I mustered up all my courage, took a deep breath, and said, "Yes. I do get free lunch." I braced for whatever being poor was going to do to our friendship.

Brad nodded and said, "Yeah, you're probably poor. Do you have a sharpener we can use for the crayons? My blue is dull."

To him, we'd solved the puzzle. It was time to move on. I wouldn't understand for years to come what a gift Brad had given me with those three sentences. He gave me the gift of acceptance and a friendship that's based on who you are instead of what you have.

In that moment, I understood two things.

One, Brad was my new favorite first-grader.

Two, if poor meant not having money, I was going to make enough money to be the exact opposite.

Realizing I couldn't fix this at school, I finished the day chomping at the bit to get home. I wanted to make a plan and put it into action. I decided I wasn't going to ask my mom about it, because if she could fix being poor, she would have done it already.

This was up to me.

When I got home from school, I was on a mission. I told my older sister I needed to make a lot of money. But I didn't want to give her too many details in case she talked to Mom when she came home from work after my bedtime.

In my eyes, the opposite of poor was rich, and rich people I knew of on TV had businesses. I started thinking of what kind of business I could start right away. I pondered the fact that I was only six, didn't have a car or bike, had no equipment or stuff to sell.

Then it hit me—I could *find* items to sell! I looked around the house and found nothing useful that I was willing to part with. Meanwhile, my sister explained I couldn't just go sell our stuff door-to-door anyway. (Had I found anything useful, I would have argued that point.)

All I found were two previously unnoticed blue markers. I put them in my pocket and went outside. I looked at the traitorous grass that had promised me riches and wished the story of Rumpelstiltskin was real. I wished I could just turn the grass into something someone would want enough to give me money for.

At that thought, inspiration struck.

Right beside all that traitorous grass was our gravel drive-way full of lots and lots of plain ol' rocks that I never gave a second glance to before. Yet now they were more than just gravel; they were the missing piece to my problem. Sure they were plain now, but I had two blue markers in my pocket, and I could make them special.

I gathered up a bunch of them in my excited little hands and yelled for my sister. Luckily, she was willing to be free labor in this new enterprise. All we had to do, I explained, was color as many rocks blue as possible. Coloring them blue would indicate they were *magic*. And anyone who had one would be able to do whatever they believed they could do.

At six, magic was still very real to me. I had been able to do anything I believed I could—even when grown-ups said I couldn't—and I was sure I could put that ability into those rocks. I was less certain my sister could, so I vowed to hold her rocks after she colored them to give them the magic.

Magic rocks. Those would be worth *a lot* of money. Who wouldn't want those?

My sister diligently helped me and, even though she colored much slower than I did, in several hours we had nearly thirty magic rocks. My hands hurt and most of my fingers were blue, but my heart was soaring.

Poor was a distant memory. We were almost rich!

The next morning, I grabbed a plastic bag we'd gotten from the grocery store and carefully put my magic rocks inside, after thoroughly inspecting them to make sure they were completely blue and had magic. I snuck the bag into my backpack, making sure to carry it myself so Mom didn't notice how heavy it was.

I decided that school was a better place for my rocks than selling to the neighbors. Grown-ups were too likely to say magic wasn't real, but kids understood that magic *is* real, it's just rare.

I priced my rocks at twenty-five cents each. My pricing strategy was based on three thoughts.

1. I liked quarters. In my opinion, they were the best change.
2. Kids at school often brought four quarters to pay for lunch, which was eighty cents.
3. Quarters added up to dollars fast. In my opinion, money adding up fast is part of what made you rich.

When Mrs. Caldwell went out of the classroom that morning, I was ready to start my business. I let everyone know I had something super special to show them: Magic Blue Rocks. I told my classmates if they had a Magic Blue Rock, they could do anything they believed they could. Anything.

I pulled the rocks out of the grocery bag in my backpack, and somehow they had transformed. They were no longer gravel colored with blue markers; they were magic totems that made your dreams come true.

Several kids gasped, and one asked, "Did they turn your fingers blue?"

I wiggled my fingers and could barely sit still in my seat. "Yes they did!"

I meant my fingers were blue from coloring the rocks. Looking back, I realize some of the kids might have seen that as proof that they were magic. They knew their moms never would've let them come to school with blue fingers if they could wash it off.

The kids crowded around me as I told them the price. Almost every single kid wanted a Magic Blue Rock—one boy wanted two! Some kids had leftover lunch money, but others only had lunch money for that day. Four quarters for an eighty-cent lunch. Most didn't think about the impact, they just wanted a Magic Blue Rock.

One girl tapped me softly on the shoulder and said so quietly I almost couldn't hear, "I won't have enough money for lunch if I buy a rock today. Can I buy one tomorrow?"

I want to say I gave her a discount.

I want to say I told her I'd hold a rock for her until tomorrow.

But I didn't.

I was on a seller's high holding all those quarters in my hand. They were the answer to the previous day's insurmountable challenge. That feeling had wiped away my shame and replaced it with a feeling of excitement I didn't fully understand.

I replied, "You don't have to buy one today, but I don't know if I'll have any rocks left tomorrow or if I'll be able to make more."

The second statement was true, since we had drained all the ink out of one of those blue markers and almost all of the second one, but it still felt a little wrong as I said it.

Another boy in our class supplied an answer for both of us: "You can buy the rock now and charge your lunch!"

That was the tipping point.

Once the kids heard they could have both the rocks *and* lunch, sales skyrocketed. I sold nearly every rock I had, one to almost every kid in class. I made more than $5 profit—a huge windfall, even after setting aside money to buy two new markers at the school bookstore.

I was in business. I had no doubt that soon I would be rich.

When lunchtime came around, I was deep into planning mode.

How many rocks could I color each night?

Could I color even more on the weekend?

Should I ask for markers for my birthday?

I was so deep in thought, I didn't see Mrs. Caldwell chatting with the lunch lady, who told her that nearly her entire class had charged their lunches because they didn't have enough money. Nor did I notice when Mrs. Caldwell talked to a few kids at the end of the lunch table while they excitedly showed her the Magic Blue Rocks they had spent their lunch money on.

Mrs. Caldwell came over and sat down beside me. "Hi, April. I've heard a great deal about your Magic Blue Rocks today."

I beamed at her. "Do you wanna buy one?"

She smiled and said in an understanding tone, "No, April. But I would love to know why you're selling rocks at school when school is for learning, not selling."

I asked to talk to Mrs. Caldwell in private. I told her what I'd found out the previous day, that I was poor, and why I thought I had to solve it myself. She was my favorite grown-up, and I felt like I could trust her.

"April, I'm going to need you to give me the rest of the rocks. I'll let you have them back when it's time to go home, as long as you promise not to sell them on the school bus."

Her words twisted my stomach until it felt like it was on fire.

My business! Where would I sell my Magic Blue Rocks?

I thought this was the worst thing she could say to me. I was wrong.

"I'm also going to need to call your mom and tell her what happened. I think she'll want to talk to you about this."

I tried to swallow but couldn't. My mom wasn't supposed to get calls at work unless it was an *emergency.* I was sure I was going to be in trouble. Plus, my whole plan had been to solve this problem and tell her when it was over. I felt that awful prickling in my nose and promised myself I Would. Not. Cry.

We went back to class, and as I tried to concentrate on my worksheet, I wondered what my mom would say to me after Mrs. Caldwell called her. Would I be in trouble because you can't sell at school? Would she be happy I thought of the solution to being poor? I could barely sit still.

"April, will you come here for a minute?"

I jumped in my seat when I heard my mom's voice.

Tingles went down my spine. My mom *never* came to school. She even had to work during parent–teacher nights! This was bad—as in bad-bad.

Mom sat down with me on a bench outside the classroom.

"April, I talked to Mrs. Caldwell about your rocks, and why you made and sold them."

I stared back at her with wide eyes.

She continued, "It's true, we don't have much money, but that's nothing to be ashamed of. Money is just something you have. It doesn't decide who you are." Her eyes welled up with tears.

I felt the shame and sadness all over again. Being poor had made my mom cry, even though she was usually so tough. Sometimes she got angry, but I couldn't remember her ever crying before. But admitting out loud that we were poor had upset her.

I knew right then and there that I would never be satisfied until we had plenty of money. I burned with the need to have enough money that talking about it didn't make us feel bad or cry or worry.

"But baby, you won't be poor when you grow up. Not because being poor is bad—it isn't. It just means you don't have a lot of money. You'll never have to worry about that because you're special. You'll be and have whatever you want."

That day changed the way I saw the world. When my mom, the strongest person I knew, talked about what I thought was a bad thing—being poor—she *cried*. When she talked about the *good thing*—that I was special and I could be whatever I wanted—her eyes shone with pride and happiness.

So I made two promises to myself at the tender age of six.

One, that I would make money until money didn't matter.

And two, I wouldn't focus on the bad that made strong people cry. I would only focus on the good that brought happiness.

My Advice

I still have more stories to share with you, but I'll tell you a secret now—it worked. I made money until money didn't matter. I did it far faster than I ever would've thought. And I did it against the odds, despite people saying I couldn't—and without any special connections or advantages.

I don't say any of that to brag. I am not smarter nor am I more special than you. I don't have more talent, and I didn't work harder than everyone else.

I simply believed.

I didn't focus on what people said I couldn't do; I focused on *what I wanted*.

The best part about this book is this—whether you have a Magic Blue Rock in your hand or not, you can do anything you believe you can.

If you're a little short on belief just now, don't worry. Keep reading.

I believe in you.

Chapter Two

ONE TRUE BELIEVER

I think all of us want someone to believe in us. Many of us don't have someone like that in our immediate family. Even when we do, our family members' mindsets and limitations can diminish their belief in us.

For much of my life, the people around me—family, friends, even strangers who happened to ask "What do you want to be when you grow up?"—often overlooked my big aspirations, gave me an odd stare, or just pretended they hadn't heard my latest pronouncement.

I didn't mind. I was planning to be the first person in my family to graduate from college, to become a TV news anchor in New York City and make enough money to buy my mom a house.

Anyone not believing only made me say it louder.

I said it over and over, thinking one day I would have no doubts whatsoever.

That worked for me, and then I found someone who believed in me even more than I believed in myself, and at the time I needed it the most.

One afternoon, I walked home from school. I opened the door and my eyes adjusted to the darkness. All the blinds were closed. Our home smelled sour, and I could hear crying in the corner. I noticed a huddled figure I knew must be my mom sitting on the far end of the couch.

The mess scared me the most. My mother was a meticulous housekeeper and demanded that it be kept pristine at all times.

My daily routine as soon as I got home from school—and before homework—consisted of vacuuming, dry dusting then spray-cleaning all the glass surfaces in the living room and dining room, then cleaning the kitchen and bathroom, including sweeping and mopping.

Skipping a day of chores was not an option, and no one would have believed this place had been spotless less than twenty-four hours before.

It looked like a hurricane had come through.

The scene before me would have normally sent prickles of fear down my back and a rush of adrenaline to my limbs, but those reactions were stopped by one person in the room who simply didn't belong.

The stranger was the tallest and most elegant woman I'd ever seen.

Dressed in beautiful, professional clothes, she had an air of calmness and kindness that reminded me of only the nicest of teachers. I was simultaneously in awe of her and immediately skeptical. I knew without a doubt that a lady as important as she obviously was didn't come to your house without a good reason.

She smiled at me warmly, held out her hand and said, "Hello, April. I'm Sue Harper. Do you remember me?"

I didn't remember her. I was sure that if we had met, I would have recognized her.

(Of course, I was also nine and had forgotten the high-level people I was instructed to wave at every year at Mom's annual company picnic, who never got more than a passing glance from me. The picnic was always at an amusement park, so all I was thinking about then was getting to the rides.)

Giving the woman a solid, confident handshake with eye contact as I'd been taught, I said, "I'm not sure."

In any other situation, I would've dived right in with, "Who are you? Why are you here? What's going on?"

Not shy at all, I always wanted to know every detail about what was happening. But something told me I wasn't going to like at least a few of those answers, so I waited for her to continue.

Sue bent down to my level with a small smile and said in a quiet voice, "I work with your mom, and I'm here to help her.

She is being very brave, April. I'm extremely proud of her, and I think you will be too."

I snuck a glance at my mom. She looked awful—unshowered, her face blotchy and puffy from hours of crying. She wouldn't even make eye contact with me.

A smell was in the air that usually warned me she'd be at her worst. I didn't know then that the smell was large amounts of alcohol being processed by her body and coming out in her sweat. All I knew was that it meant I had to be very good and very careful or bad things would happen.

I looked back at Sue wide-eyed. I was confused. I didn't see anything I was proud of in this apartment.

"She's going to go to a place called CADAS for a little while, where they help people who have drinking problems. Do you know your mom has a drinking problem?"

I swallowed. Did I? I knew our situation was bad. I knew I wasn't supposed to talk about it. I knew my mom was terrifying to me most of the time, and it seemed to be getting worse. She was so unpredictable. No matter how hard I tried, I couldn't be good enough to keep her from hitting me.

Oh but I definitely tried. When she'd get home from work, I'd make sure I'd done all of my chores, had kept all the vacuum lines straight, and had not walked on any of them before she could see.

If she was in a good mood, I'd make a list of accomplishments to tell her about to make her proud, and if she wasn't, a plan to busy myself out of her sight.

Sometimes I'd go to a friend's house after school, but I'd soon realized that wasn't a good idea because I wasn't there to greet her when she got home. Even though I always left a note saying when I'd be back, she'd often be furious. She'd find fault in the way I cleaned a table, or stew because I wasn't there to answer a question she had. Whatever it was, if I wasn't there to fix it, her temper got worse and bad things happened.

Also, my mom, who'd always been known as the hardest worker at any job she had, was missing work more and more.

On workdays, she'd normally be gone before I got up to get ready for school. Every once in a while though, she'd wake me a little early with bunny kisses on the side of my face singing, "Good morning, sunshine. The earth says hello!"

She would gently put my hair behind my ear with her fingers and hand me a special breakfast—a sliced tomato-and-cheese sandwich with a little bit of mayonnaise, which never tasted the same when I made it.

I couldn't remember the last time she'd woken me up that way.

What I did remember, more and more often, was my nervousness. I'd come downstairs to that awful sour smell, Mom sprawled out on the sofa, unmoving and unwakeable even as the phone rang. I knew the call was from her boss at the factory wondering where she was.

Picking up the phone, I'd tell him as I'd been instructed: "I'm sorry, my mom is very sick, and she won't be in today." I could always tell he wanted to ask me more questions, and I was always so grateful that he didn't.

I was a bad liar.

In a way, she was sick, but I knew enough to know she wasn't the kind of sick that makes it okay to miss work. So it twisted my stomach in knots to pretend that she was.

My mind whirled with memories and experiences that seemed so much bigger and worse than the words "drinking problem." I was both grateful that Sue Harper didn't ask about what I knew, and a little disappointed that so many awful events were supposed to fit in that tiny explanation.

So when she asked me whether I knew my mother had a problem, I nodded.

"The good news, April, is that your mom is going to fix it," Sue explained. "She's going to get well, and that's going to make your life much, much better." She took my hand and bent down to be closer to my height.

Though I'd been brave and stoic in my fear, the sympathy and kindness in her gesture and her words caused me to break down. My eyes flooded with tears, and I asked in a small voice cracking from the lump in my throat, "How long will she be gone?"

"It's a program that takes about a month," Sue explained. "Twenty-eight days. We've already spoken to your aunt, and she will take care of you until your mom gets back."

I was overwhelmed. This was so weird. It seemed terrible, yet this smart and impressive lady was telling me it was good.

My mom was leaving me *for a month*. Even though living with her was scary, I didn't want her to go!

I loved my aunt and enjoyed staying with her, but she worked second shift at the factory, and my little cousin went to a baby-sitter. Would I be alone all the time? I felt like nothing would ever be the same.

Then there was Mom. She was just sitting on the sofa crying and letting Sue Harper talk to me about the big secret I was supposed to hide.

It was like a bad dream when you don't know that you're dreaming so you can't stop it or turn it around somehow.

Except then Sue Harper did turn it around.

"April, I know this is hard, and it's a lot for you to think about right now. I'd like to ask you a favor, okay? I would like you to trust me. I have helped a lot of families this way."

She continued, "Our company believes in giving people second chances, and your mom needs one of those. If I promise you that her completing this program will make both of your lives better, do you feel like you can believe in that?"

I did. Though I didn't know why I did.

Sue was so trustworthy, so together, so different than any other grown-up I'd ever met in my life. By that point, I was no longer willing to bet on my mom.

Too many times I'd been shown that I couldn't rely on her, but I was willing to bet on Sue Harper.

"I believe you," I said. "Tell me what I need to do, and I'll do it!"

Sue smiled and hugged me.

She told me she'd stay with me until my aunt came, and then take my mom right to the place called CADAS. She said I wouldn't be able to see my mom for a few weeks, and then after that only for short periods of time until she finished the program.

She asked me to be brave and told me I could hug my mom before they left.

Then she made one last statement.

"You're special, April. SO special. I can see all the wonderful things you're going to be able to do. And I want to be your friend. You can call me when you need someone to talk to, and I will be there for you. I'd love to be a part of your life."

She could have knocked me over with a feather.

The most awe-inspiring person I had ever met in my life thought I was special and would do wonderful things!

It was a turning point that even I didn't recognize.

Truthfully, I'd always thought what Sue had just said was true. I hadn't paid much attention when people scoffed at my big dreams, because I figured they just didn't get it.

Everyone who surrounded me said, "People like us don't go to college." I fought the urge to yell out loud, "I do! I'm not like you!"

Instead, I let those words echo in my head and repeated often to myself, "I'm different. *I will*."

Here was someone who was better than anyone I knew who had a life I'd like to have telling me that it was true!

I knew even back then that you weren't supposed to think anyone was better than anyone else, but I didn't have the right words to describe the difference between "someone you'd like to be like" and "someone who served as a cautionary tale."

"I would love that," I said, with my first smile of the day.

Then I asked for her phone number and address.

Some of my normal April-ness was returning. Let's get this friendship nailed down and on the books!

The time Mom was in rehab seemed like forever, and it was hard. Once she realized that her *not drinking* was a step in the right direction but not a total cure for her struggles, that was even harder for us both.

However, no difficulty could overshadow the light that had entered my life in the form of Sue Harper. She supported my mom in her sobriety like she did with all the employees the company helped through its drug and alcohol treatment program. Sue helped start the program and facilitated it as the head of human resources.

From my perspective, she was everything she had promised and more.

Her generosity with her time and attention was the stuff of legend. It was also the inspiration for The Generosity Culture®, a business philosophy that I would create decades later to help scale and turn around businesses across the globe.

She became my "Aunt Sue," attending my school events and even traveling to see me speak when I started entering speech contests. She sent me encouraging cards and gave me advice while she served as a beacon to the life I planned to have.

Her belief in me fueled me while also helping me prepare to be who I wanted to be.

My dream—in addition to all the other dreams—was to some-day have the honor of being someone else's "Sue Harper."

Now more than thirty years later, Aunt Sue is still one of my closest friends and a very special part of my life.

In her late eighties, she still hops onto her computer so we can email back and forth, still has better penmanship than me, and is always on my visit list when I go back to Tennessee. I'm grateful that she can see how her act of generosity in befriend-ing and pouring wisdom into me has touched so many lives beyond mine.

Sue would tell you that she didn't do anything special that day. She'd say she offered me what she offered to any child in that situation. I just grabbed ahold of it.

We should all aspire to have our regular, ordinary actions be so generous and loving that they change lives in ways we can't even imagine. We should also remember that our dark-est times and biggest struggles often put us in the perfect place for the best thing that could ever happen to us.

In many cases, I don't believe it's possible to have one with-out the other.

My Advice

People have asked me over the years if I wish my childhood had been different.

Absolutely not.

That experience brought me many things that have made my life amazing, including Sue Harper.

Knowing now that one of the best things in my life was preceded by some of the worst allows me to look at hard situations much differently. I feel them like everyone else and want them to speed by (hey, I'm human!), but I also trust that they are working *for* me instead of happening *to* me. Like me, I encourage you to focus on the excitement of knowing hard times will bring you another amazing thing that, in hindsight, you'd never be willing to trade for not experiencing the tough thing.

It can be hard to do sometimes, but I promise it's worth it.

Even if you think you can't, don't worry.

I know you can.

Chapter Three

DING-DONG, AVON CALLING!

Though selling Magic Blue Rocks was my first business, it wasn't my last.

I spent my childhood dreaming of future careers, success, and wealth. Money seemed like the answer to every question, problem, or challenge.

Early on, I understood that money was powerful, because it was always a topic of conversation in my home. More accurately, the idea of "enough money" rather than just money itself. The conversation was often, "Will we have enough money to pay the rent? When will we have enough money to turn the electricity back on? Can we afford to get groceries this week?"

By the time I was twelve, we rented a nicer home, thanks to my mom's factory job. It even had a washer and dryer, which was a huge deal for us. We didn't have a car at the time, and that worried my mom and kept her perpetually angry at my out-of-work stepdad.

For me, the number one concern was my wardrobe. Specifically, clothes nice enough to help me blend in at school where most of the kids were much better off than we were.

Thanks to Brad, I had guarded the secret that I was poor like the government guards state secrets. It was on a need-to-know basis—and in my mind, *no one* needed to know.

Middle-school kids were hard to fool.

Free-lunch tickets in middle school were a different color than regular lunch tickets, making them stand out even more. I was terrified of being made fun of and labeled. I was so worried that I chose not to eat lunch at all. On the rare occasion a teacher noticed me not eating, I would say I'd had a big breakfast or had a bellyache.

It was harder to find a solution for the clothing problem. Anyone who's gone to a school that doesn't require uniforms knows that there are clothes and shoes that are "cool" and those that aren't. The cool clothes usually come with name brands and a higher price tag. They also come with a type of acceptance that kids truly want but often can't convey to their parents. I know I sure couldn't.

Besides the fact that my mom couldn't afford to buy those clothes for me, she also saw brand obsession as "materialistic and shallow." She counseled me to be a better person than that. She was all for me working and earning money but much preferred when I used it to pay for school supplies, field trips, or activities with my friends. Using that money for nicer clothes was a waste in her eyes. She told me that over and over.

What I never said out loud—and maybe didn't even understand myself—was that I saw nicer clothes as armor.

I thought they would protect me from other kids knowing our secrets. That my mom—although now sober—was still often mean and unpredictable, and sometimes violent. That my parents fought more often than they didn't. That my sister had a disability and lived with my grandmother.

My mom thought I wanted to hide the fact that we were poor, but it was so much more than that. I truly believed we were different from other people—*less than* other people—and I didn't want anyone to know.

When I reflect on how afraid I was for the other kids to know about my family and circumstances, my heart breaks a little to know that there were probably other children just like me who bore the same burden. Maybe they still do today because they don't realize that no family is "normal." There are so many people who would understand and accept them, even when that's the hardest thing for them to imagine at the time.

I didn't ponder the bigger meaning of any of this back then. I only saw the simple problem of needing nicer clothes to fit in. All I needed to solve this problem was money. In my view, there was plenty of it out there—I just had to find ways to earn it.

So simple, right?

By this point, I'd been doing some odd jobs for a couple of years. I would mostly babysit (back when trusting adults would leave their young children with a mature ten-year-old without a thought). I'd also worked a paper route with limited success. The newspapers wanted people who had cars and could deliver hundreds of papers twice a day.

At the age of twelve, I was on the search for a great summer job that would help me make lots of money. Specifically, I needed work that didn't require a car or driver's license—or for me to be of legal working age.

I could get a special hardship worker's permit, but not until I was fourteen, which was two long years away. But I had a plan: I had the help wanted ads from the newspaper, the telephone, and the house to myself for the afternoon.

I could figure this out.

As you can imagine, there weren't many jobs that fit my criteria. Most of them were office positions that I knew wouldn't hire me and required skills I didn't have. A few jobs that fit were less than appealing.

Technically, I could spend my summer as a "yard laborer," but since one of my regular chores was to mow our lawn each week—and extra yard work was the punishment of choice for when I chose to "speak my mind"—doing that sounded like torture.

Then I found it! It was the perfect job for me.

The ad read: "Be your own boss...flexible hours, training provided, and unlimited earning potential. Become an Avon Representative today!"

I'd heard of Avon. I had seen the catalogs at my grandmother's house. I loved the idea of having my own business selling products I didn't have to create. Makeup seemed easy to sell because every lady I knew wore it.

I made the phone call, planning to use my most businesslike voice. When the nice-sounding lady answered, I stated with confidence, "Hello, I'm April. I saw your ad in the paper for Avon representatives, and I think I'd be perfect."

To my surprise, she sounded more excited than I was.

She told me she was looking to grow her team, and I was the first person to answer the ad. She asked me what my goals were and why I wanted to work for Avon.

I answered, "I want to make as much money as possible, and I'm willing to work hard to do it. I chose Avon because of your ad, and because I think a lot of people will buy from me."

Those people were the older ladies in my neighborhood. I knew they would want free samples of lipstick and for me to spend time talking to them at their houses. I also knew a lot of women at my mom's factory. They bought from me every year when my school was selling candy or wrapping paper, so I had no doubt they'd be willing to buy Avon.

The lady on the phone was thrilled. She said Avon sounded like a good fit for me because the more I sold, the more they would pay me. I would get forty percent off the products if I sold a certain amount. She said Avon would give me even more of a discount for large orders, all of which would be my profit/income.

She mentioned that normally representatives would have to purchase a starter kit, but she was giving them away for free to the first three people she signed up, which included me.

I tried to quell my excitement and sound professional, but I was jumping up and down as I listened to her explain how the sales and ordering process would work.

She took down all my information to mail me the starter kit: full name, address, and phone number to start. I held my breath, worrying she'd ask for my birthdate, but she didn't.

We were almost done when she inquired, "Do you have any questions before we make this official?"

That sounded serious, so I thought I should make sure my age wasn't an issue.

"Well," I said, "I want to make sure the company would be okay with a younger person selling, since most of the Avon ladies I've known have been older."

"Oh absolutely," she responded. "We love the idea of younger representatives who want a long career with Avon."

"Awesome!" I said, then quickly wondered if businesswomen ever said "awesome." I made a mental note to ask Aunt Sue the next time we talked. I said thank you and goodbye, and hung up.

I immediately ran around the house looking for a calculator. I spent the next hour thinking of amounts of larger and larger Avon orders and then doing the math to see how much profit I would make.

What if I made as much money as Mom did at the factory? My dreams of nicer clothes quickly blossomed into a car for the family, a college education, and what it would be like to have so much money that money didn't matter.

I felt amazing!

I told Mom about my new venture when she got home.

She asked if they knew I was twelve. She accepted my response that the lady thought I was *very mature* and that they were trying to hire younger people.

She said, "April, you know it takes money to make money. You're going to have to *buy* the products to *sell* them to other people, and I can't help you."

First, I thought that was the silliest saying ever. You wouldn't need to *make money* if you already *had money*. I chalked it up to one of those weird comments adults say with authority that don't actually make sense.

"Mom, Avon is genius," I retorted. "I don't have to pay for the products before I sell them. I get people's orders, place them with Avon, then they send the products and an invoice. Then I have two weeks to pay the invoice, which is plenty of time to deliver the orders and get the money. I keep my part and send Avon their part."

I was so confident, I threw in a final, "I don't need money to make money. I just have to put in the work!"

She raised an eyebrow at me but didn't respond.

Mom and I had fundamentally different outlooks. She was always expecting something to go wrong. In her experience, it always did. I always expected life to work out perfectly. In my experience, if it didn't, it was a fluke.

My Avon kit came quickly. I got to work right away making little bags of catalogs with the perfect samples. I would take these to the older women in the neighborhood, and my mom would take them to her friends at work.

Mom said not to count on a lot of orders because the women at the factory weren't going to want to buy Avon all the time. I just smiled and asked her to give them my catalogs. Once again, I had a plan.

It was simple: I would make people feel special, and they'd want to buy from me. I wanted to buy nicer clothes because they would make me feel good, and I thought other people probably bought makeup for similar reasons. It was worth a shot.

I knew my mom's coworkers well. I made special bags of catalogs and samples for each of them, labeled with their names. I included colors that would look good on each person based on my Avon charts.

I also used any information that my mom had shared about them to choose samples they'd find value in. I wrote them little notes like, "Sandy, Mom said you hate when the baby keeps you up at night because you get bags under your eyes when you don't get enough sleep. Try this eye cream sample. It says it's perfect for that!"

It was more effort than the drop-off-catalogs-everywhere-with-a-few-samples process my manager had told me about, but it worked exceptionally well. Those wonderful ladies ordered from me each and every Avon campaign (what Avon called the two-week period when a new catalog was out).

I had a similar plan for the older women in my neighborhood: I would customize samples and spend time with them. Many of the women had shared with me that no one ever sat down and talked with them anymore now that they were retired. Everyone was too busy. I combined our Avon visits with conversations about their grandkids, families, animals, and whatever else they wanted to talk about.

It was a win-win.

They felt valued sharing stories about their lives and teaching me, and I had new friends and sales! The best part was seeing those new friends (my neighborhood ladies) wearing that bright red lipstick they couldn't resist buying and how they were inspired to dress up because of it.

My business brought new energy into their lives and a lot of fun and learning into mine.

Life was amazing.

I made enough sales to buy school clothes and to help with some home expenses. Surprisingly, I also found out from my manager that I was going to be recognized at our district sales meeting! Though I hadn't been selling long enough to get an actual award, my manager said she'd asked our district manager to recognize how quickly I had grown my business in our district.

This was big.

I didn't have a suit, so I wore my nicest dress, a hand-me-down from one of my cousins that still looked brand-new and made me feel very grown-up.

It was a sheath dress, brown with cream-colored polka dots. It was a different dress style, but the exact same pattern as the one Julia Roberts had worn in the famous polo match scene in *Pretty Woman*. I paired the dress with cream-colored pumps (with a tiny heel) and my Avon bag, and I felt every bit as fancy as she had looked in the movie.

I was looking forward to meeting my manager in person, because we'd only spoken by phone.

I walked into the building for the meeting and saw a lot of folding chairs, women milling around the room chatting— some in business attire, but most completely casual—and a few snacks and coffee on a side table.

I looked to the front of the room, hoping to see a lectern and a microphone, or anything that would signal this was a business meeting. I was greeted by folding tables covered in vinyl tablecloths normally reserved for kids' birthday parties. They unceremoniously displayed the new products the district manager was going to show us.

Where was the conference table full of women wearing power suits sitting in leather chairs making huge business decisions?

I vowed to myself that when I was a district manager, we would make these gatherings much fancier. Then I scanned the crowd for the nice lady who had hired me.

When I found her (she told me what she'd be wearing), I walked right up to her. During a slight pause in her conversation with another guest, I said, "Hi, I'm April!"

My manager politely wrapped up her conversation, then turned to me and said, "I'm sorry, I missed what you said. Did you say you're here with April? Are you her daughter?"

"No." I laughed. "I AM April!"

Her eyes widened.

I thought maybe she wasn't expecting me to look so professional. Actually, what she wasn't expecting was for me to be a child.

"April, how old are you?" she asked as politely as she could while still trying to hide her shock.

"I turned thirteen last month," I said, offering my best hand-shake with a big smile. I was so glad I was no longer twelve. A teenager selling Avon made a lot more sense than a twelve-year-old, even to me.

"Wow," she responded with a half grin that didn't reach her surprise-filled eyes. Speaking slowly as if her mind was going a mile a minute it took her a couple beats too long to accept my outstretched hand. "I had no idea you were so young! Now I'm even more amazed at how much you've sold."

She didn't look amazed; she looked like she'd just found out she'd accidentally baked her award-winning apple pie with salt instead of sugar as the judge took his first bite. For the first time since my phone interview, I worried that my age *was* going to be an issue.

She told me she'd let the district manager know I was there and to have a seat because the meeting was about to start.

I chose a seat where I could see the entire room and watched my manager speed-walk up to the professional-looking woman at the front of the room. My manager was talking a mile a minute as she waved her hands around anxiously and then nodded toward me.

The district manager followed her gaze and looked directly into my eyes.

I smiled, trying to slow my racing heart, forced myself to hold eye contact, and gave a little wave.

Though her eyes had widened the tiniest bit when she saw me, she didn't miss a beat. She gave me a single nod with an impressed expression on her face.

It wasn't all the assurance I wanted in that moment, but I breathed a sigh of relief with that small positive sign.

The district manager started the meeting. She shared valuable information and then took us through all the new products. In my excitement about the neat new things, I forgot all about my age concern. Avon had come out with new fragrances, makeup, jewelry, and what my district manager called "the biggest breakthrough," a moisturizing cream for your neck and chest with SPF to keep the skin from losing elasticity and getting sun damage.

"Ladies, we all know how key it is to take care of our décolletage. Well, except perhaps our youngest *outstanding* representative, who I'm going to be recognizing for sales growth today. April, it might not seem pressing now, but protect that skin on your chest and you'll look young forever."

I beamed at her, feeling like a true member of the team.

(By the way, I've never forgotten that advice. And just as she said, I didn't think it mattered…until I was old enough to wish I had!)

After the meeting, my manager asked me to come with her to talk to our district manager. When we walked up, she greeted us warmly.

"April, you're a first for us. We've never had someone your age want to work with us, much less prove to be so successful." She continued her supportive vibe by letting me know, "According to Avon's rules, a representative should be an adult, but there's no rule that says an adult can't sign up for you and let you sell under their name. Do you think one of your parents would do that for you?"

I said yes without knowing for certain they would, but not seeing why they wouldn't. I was making real money with this business!

"Wonderful. I think we're going to see great things from you," she said warmly.

"I promise you will," I gushed back.

After that meeting, I continued to sell to my client base and had steady growth for the next few months. But I wanted *more*.

I needed new customers. I needed people I didn't already know. That need introduced me to an area of sales where I struggled, like lots of others had before me—cold calling.

I didn't have much luck when I just rang doorbells at strangers' houses and asked to come in with my Avon bag. So I tried leaving them samples and catalogs in bags hanging on their front doorknobs. I hoped they'd love the tiny gifts and call me to place an order, or at the very least be willing to chat when I came back. I'd excitedly walk up to house after house on my return visits a few days later, only to find the bags of goodies still hanging on the front doors.

There had to be a way to get them to notice the catalog and samples.

I thought of putting a bow on each bag to make it stand out, but threw the idea out when I noticed how many people were entering their houses through the garage. They rarely used their front doors.

I needed the bags to be somewhere people looked *every day* so they'd get them right away.

Then it hit me. I was surprised I hadn't thought of it before.

Their mailboxes! Everyone checked mail every day (this was pre-internet and online bills), and they paid attention to what was in the mailbox.

I put my new plan into action immediately, filling as many mailboxes as I could walk to each day with sample bags and catalogs, and then waited for the calls.

And they came!

I had many calls from soon-to-be new clients…and one from the postmaster. My mom picked up his call. Our mail carrier informed her that I was regularly committing a *federal crime*.

Oops!

He had easily figured out I had been the one leaving the bags in everyone's mailboxes within a two-mile radius, because my name and phone number were stamped on the catalogs. He wasn't able to catch any of us at home to tell me to stop, however. Since using federal property such as mailboxes to hold items that weren't US mail was illegal, he had to try another route to end my life of crime.

Mom couldn't believe I didn't know that I wasn't allowed to put my catalogs in mailboxes. And I couldn't believe the post office didn't see the revenue opportunity of allowing people to use mailboxes for items other than mail.

I'd happily pay to have a place where my catalogs and samples would be easily noticed. My mom pointed out the way to do that was to pay to mail them. Valid point, but too rich for my blood. So I was out of the mailbox game.

I continued to work on new customer-acquisition strategies. Meanwhile, the way Avon allowed me to do business worked really well for me. The time they gave me between receiving an order and having to pay my invoice (out of the customers' payments) allowed my business to grow bigger and bigger without needing any capital to buy the products. I had campaign after campaign with lots of orders from my customers.

One delivery day, I'd prepped all my samples, notes, and bags on my bedroom floor. I was ready to start the packing process once all the products arrived.

But they didn't.

Shipments had always arrived on the same day of the week. Yet on that particular day, UPS didn't show up. I waited until my bedtime…and still nothing. I decided to call Avon as soon as I woke up the next morning.

Unfortunately, Avon didn't open before school started, so I had to ask for permission to call them from the school office. The Avon rep said that all of my products had shipped and that they should be at my house already. They gave me the tracking number so I could call UPS and check on it. I'd never called them before, but it seemed like a great idea to get to the bottom of this. Unfortunately, tracking packages wasn't as easy then as it is now.

The office secretary said I should call when I got home because I'd be on hold for a while. I went back to class and prayed that the box would be at my door when I got home.

It wasn't.

I was really getting worried. I usually had plenty of time to deliver orders and collect money to pay my invoice, but my products had never come late before.

After twenty-five minutes on hold, I finally got through to UPS. They said my package was lost. They said that often when this happens, the package shows up within a couple of weeks.

I was panicked. I didn't have a couple of weeks!

I called my manager and asked for advice. She said I had two options. One was to wait for the package, which would probably show up within the next few days to a week. The other option was to reorder all the items.

Option two would require me, for the first time, to pay my invoice *before* they'd extend me credit to place another order. I could then return the first order when it showed up for a credit on a future order. But if the products didn't show up, or if they took longer, I would have to pay out of my own pocket and make a claim with UPS to get the money back.

I felt like I was going to be sick.

I was in no way prepared for this situation. I hadn't saved *any* of the money I'd made over the six months I was working. I'd paid for school clothes, fees, and supplies I needed. I'd taken my family out to dinner a few times, and I'd bought a dresser for my bedroom. I'd invested money back into the business by buying catalogs and samples, but that investment was a small amount of money compared to what I'd earned.

I'd blown it.

My invoice would be more than $500 plus shipping charges for my $900 in sales. That was as much as our monthly rent!

I had no idea how I would get that kind of money or who I would get it from.

Since both options required my customers to wait longer for their orders, I decided to go with option one, and I'd wait and pray my order got there quickly. If it didn't, I would have to find a way to pay the invoice until I could claim insurance with UPS on the package. I thought maybe I would see if Avon would work with me to allow me to pay my invoice when I got the insurance refund.

I would have loved to order for my customers again, but I knew it would take me time to figure out how to get that money. I was heartbroken.

Over the next several days, I made calls and visited my customers. I explained the situation as positively as I could, telling them their orders were delayed and that I'd get them as soon as possible.

In the meantime, my mom told me I had to figure out the money situation. If the products didn't come, she couldn't help me. Her anger and disappointment in me was palpable.

She didn't say, "I told you so," but I could feel it every time we talked about "this mess you got yourself into."

After racking my brain for options for almost a week, I made a difficult call to my grandmother. She was the only person I knew who had a credit card. I asked her if I could use it to pay my invoice if I didn't get my products in time. I promised to pay it back with the insurance money, plus interest.

I was in tears. I felt like such a failure.

But Grandma said, "April, people in our family have done far worse for dumber reasons. No need for tears. I will help you, and you will be fine."

I hoped with all I had that she was right.

She was. The next day, my products came…twelve days late. I was so relieved!

My invoice was due right away, so I hustled to get all my customers their orders and collect payment (minus shipping costs, since their orders were so late).

However, after weeks of waiting for their products, many of my customers no longer wanted them. I was sad but I understood.

I walked home with my head hung low, thinking about all the products I'd have to return to Avon. This made my overall sales lower, which greatly lowered my earnings percentage. Between that fiasco and the free shipping I'd given everyone, I was at *zero profit* for that campaign. Instead of going out with a bang, I went out with a thud.

As soon as I paid the invoice, my mom made me shut down the business. She forbade me from starting any more businesses until I was out of the house. She said it wasn't worth the stress.

I could tell she considered the whole venture a failure. What could go wrong had gone wrong.

Yes I failed. I failed *epically*. But I'd also built a business as a thirteen-year-old. And I learned a great lesson about planning and saving money, which stayed with me for life. And things going wrong...was a fluke!

My Advice

What I want you to take from this story is this: failure teaches powerful lessons.

I've been able to help many companies improve and turn their businesses around by using the very principles of preparation, planning, and risk analysis that I stumbled over back then. I feel lucky to have learned so young and with minimal damage…unless you count my teenage pride!

The biggest learning I had from this is that while there are all sorts of rules in the world, there are also many possible exceptions.

As I've mentioned before, I'm not any more special than you. This means you're absolutely able (and I think destined) to be the exception too. Always be willing to politely and confidently ask for that exception. You'll be shocked at how often people say yes.

Chapter Four

WORKING 9 TO 5

"Face it, April. You'll never make as much as I do because you're a woman," Chauncey said with a cocky grin.

He leaned into the counter where I was counting my tips. I was counting furiously, hoping they'd add up to the number he'd shared or more.

I narrowed my eyes. "Isn't it sexist to say that?" I was actually much more frustrated by him always beating me in tips than the nonsense he often spoke.

He laughed. "No, it'd be sexist if I said I was a better server than you because I'm a man. But I didn't, because you're much better than me. You're just too irritated to see the logic."

He was right, I *was* irritated. I'd worked at this steakhouse for nearly six months, learning every skill, putting my heart and soul into my service, but Chauncey *still* beat me in tips whenever we worked together, no matter what. He was easily in the bottom twenty-five percent of us service-wise yet still made so much, which hurt my soul.

He continued with his "coaching," whether I wanted it or not. "You have to understand the angle and work it, April. It's far more common for a woman to wait on people than a man in the Deep South. That's *my* angle."

I rolled my eyes. "You're lazy. You don't even take care of your customers."

His cocky grin made another appearance. "Which is why I love the nights you work. I make even more! You care so much about the diners' experience, you make sure they have what they need whether they're yours or not."

"It's cute," he added, managing to sound both complimentary *and* condescending.

I heaved a sigh trying to hide my frustration. "You don't even care that you didn't earn the extra tips, do you?"

"Why would I? The women tip me more because I'm a novelty. The men tip me more because I'm a man, or because they feel sorry for me. Who cares? I'm the one making more money than I've made doing any other job, and I basically just have to show up and smile."

Chauncey grated on my last nerve.

I believed so fully in hard work and effort being the way to get ahead. Pretty much everything about him flew in the face of that.

As irritating as he was, I reminded myself that I could learn from anyone. That said, I'd already learned from Chauncey that the few dollars it cost to dry-clean my uniform shirt outweighed the hours it would take to launder, starch, and iron it to perfection. I wasn't sure he had any more wisdom than that to offer.

"You believe too much in hard work, April. You should find a situation where you have a natural advantage and milk it." He checked his watch. "Speaking of a natural advantage, I'm late for my date."

He didn't do any of the cleaning or side work the rest of us had to do because he'd paid one of the other servers to do it for him with his extra tips.

As I did my work, to perfection because I really thought it mattered, I thought about what Chauncey had said. There was a nugget in there, I was sure, even though he was a lazy twenty-two-year-old who weirdly went by his last name like a high school football player.

I liked interacting with people—it was easy to get hired, and there were always extra shifts to make extra money. But as much as I appreciated working in the service industry, he was right. It wasn't where I had a natural advantage.

My natural advantage was in business. Two shut-down-by-an-adult businesses notwithstanding, I believed I'd be far more successful in an office than at a restaurant.

The question was, what type of office?

I pondered that on my drive home and while I tried to fall sleep. I told myself I'd be brimming with ideas in the morning. But I wasn't.

Luckily, it was a Saturday, and I was overdue to clean my room. While organizing my desk, I saw a recent card from Aunt Sue.

Aunt Sue worked at an office. As a matter of fact, she was in charge of all the hiring for the entire company. I figured surely a mentor who believed in you was a good place to start, so I called her and, without giving any details, asked if I could come see her at work on Monday.

I spent all weekend practicing my speech, updating my resume (thank goodness we'd learn to create them in typing class), and brainstorming ways I could be useful at Synthetic Industries, the factory and office where my mom and Aunt Sue worked.

On Monday, I wore my most professional dress and brought my resume in a manila folder. When I arrived, I said hello to Rosie (the receptionist of thirty-plus years) as if I were a real job applicant instead of a factory worker's daughter who'd known and loved her since I was eight. Basically, that meant I didn't run behind her desk and give her a hug.

She seemed to recognize that I was going for "grown-up," so she told me, "I'll let Mrs. Harper know you're here, ma'am," and then winked.

I was really nervous waiting for Aunt Sue in the lobby.

What if she thought it was silly that I wanted an office job?

What if she didn't think I was qualified?

Honestly, I wasn't sure I *was* qualified, but I was sure I *could* be if someone would show me what to do.

My fears and affirmations were stopped in their tracks as Aunt Sue stepped out of her office with a smile and called, "April?"

I waited until her office door was closed and we'd both sat down before I put my resume on her desk and my words came out in a rush.

"Hi, Aunt Sue! I'm here because I'd really like to work in a professional job and I can type 120 words per minute and file well and I'm prompt and friendly and have a great telephone demeanor and I'll work harder than anyone you've ever met what do you think?"

That was not the speech I had planned. Well it was the basic information, but I didn't realize I'd open my mouth and spit it all out like an auctioneer.

Aunt Sue smiled. She still had that kind, calming way about her that made me feel like I was exactly where I should be doing exactly the right thing, even when I knew I had just made a fool of myself.

"April, I think it's fantastic that you want to work in business. I also think you'd be great at it. But I can't just hire you full-time when we don't have a position open. That would be abusing my role here."

I felt my stomach tighten, preparing me for the sting of rejection.

Aunt Sue continued, "What I can do is hire you for a temp position for two weeks, starting a couple weeks from now."

I didn't know what that meant, unless it was short for "temporary," but that didn't stop me from saying, "I'll take it!"

Sue smiled again. "Rhonda, the assistant to the vice president of marketing is going on a one-week vacation. You can fill in for her by scheduling meetings, answering phones, typing, and filing. Once Rhonda is back, you can float to other administrative areas that need help."

It all sounded good to me.

"I can only pay you $6 an hour, our starting wage, because you don't have previous experience."

Now $6 an hour was $1.75 more than minimum wage at the time. If I worked full-time for the summer, I could earn just as much as I did at the steakhouse. It might be more hours, but it was in my element.

I beamed and said, "Okay!"

Leaning forward, Sue smiled back. "I can't hire you for a position that doesn't exist, April, but that doesn't mean you can't create one for yourself. Wayne, the vice president of marketing, is well thought of here. Do a good job for him and show everyone you work with how special you are. If you can let them see in you what I already see in you, I feel confident you'll be able to stay."

"I will, Aunt Sue. I'll make you proud!" And I meant it with all my heart.

I walked out of that office so excited, I think I floated all the way to my car. My mom had allowed me to buy the car from her for only $400 so I could get to work and high school. I knew what a gift that was, though I was more excited now than on the day I got it. Mom had paid $1,000 for it only six months before and now, without a vehicle, she had to catch a ride with friends to work because she'd sold it to me.

Instead of driving home, I went straight to the steakhouse to deliver my written resignation and two weeks' notice in person. It was also in my manila folder, because I had planned for success.

Some folks might think that quitting my server job before I knew whether I'd be able to get a full-time position at Synthetic Industries was foolish. They might be right. That said, I had logic behind my actions.

In the eighth grade, I had learned about Hernán Cortés and his conquest of the Aztecs in 1519. My history teacher had us hold a trial for Cortés to defend his actions. The teacher made me the defense attorney, but I really wanted to be the prosecuting attorney. I thought Cortés was *absolutely* guilty of crimes against the Aztecs, but my teacher wouldn't allow us to trade roles.

Since I also wanted to win the case for the extra credit, I studied Cortés's story in great detail while trying to find a strategy for his defense. The studying didn't change my opinion of his guilt, but it did teach me a valuable lesson about being "all in."

Cortés, in his conquest for Mexico, had his men burn the boats at the start of the battle, so retreat was not an option. His actions had assured they would try their hardest to win. And they succeeded.

As much as I didn't like him, that idea of burning the boats always stuck with me.

Incidentally, I won the history class court case, even though the student chosen as the prosecuting attorney had the fantastic idea to call witnesses. She brought up survivors, who described in great detail the horror of what Cortés had done to their families, saying they'd never forget. The strategy was brilliant and should have won her the case.

It would have had it not given me the idea to whisper to a boy beside me that *he* was Cortés and to only stand up when I asked for Hernán Cortés to identify himself.

On cross-examination, I asked the witnesses to identify their attacker out of the fifteen or so boys in the classroom. When they couldn't, I asked "Hernán Cortés" to stand, proving he was not who they were talking about. I then moved for the judge (our teacher) to dismiss all charges, which he did. (Thank you, *L.A. Law!*)

So while it may have seemed a little rash to deliver my resignation before I'd solidified a position at Synthetic Industries, doing so made it more likely I'd be able to secure one. I was burning the boats.

The icing on the cake was walking into the steakhouse to talk to the manager and seeing Chauncey starting his shift. Seeing my professional clothes, he asked me if I had gone to traffic court.

"No," I said, with my own cocky grin. "I'm delivering my resignation and two weeks' notice. I was hired today to be the assistant to the vice president of marketing at Synthetic Industries. Business is an area where I have more of a natural advantage."

Chauncey gaped at me.

I smirked and walked away.

Yes I was smug.

Yes I should've been a bigger person.

No I'm not sorry.

Working as a temporary employee for Synthetic Industries was so much fun! Wayne, the vice president of marketing, was very kind and very serious. He gave me a detailed explanation of what he needed from me and let me know that the other assistant in Marketing, Peggy, could help answer any other questions I had.

Peggy was in her early forties, serious, quiet, and professional. While she wasn't unfriendly, she seemed both shy and reluctant to chat. I took that to either mean we weren't supposed to talk a lot in the office or that she had a lot of work to do—it was Monday, after all. I decided to keep quiet and work on my tasks until I figured out which it was.

Other than the fact that the company assistants used PCs instead of the Apple computers I'd learned to use at school (causing me a little learning curve), it was really easy. Besides answering the phones and scheduling any meetings for Wayne in his paper calendar, I finished all the work I had to do for the day about two hours after I had started.

I thought surely Rhonda's job was more complicated than this, but also assumed they had given me the bare minimum amount of work as a fill-in employee so I didn't mess up anything crucial.

Peggy, on the other hand, was swamped with work. She and I had adjoining offices. Her phone rang off the hook, she was busily creating a marketing presentation, and folks kept coming in to ask her questions about every fifteen minutes.

During a quiet moment, I stepped into her office and said, "Peggy, I've pretty much run out of work. Is there something I can do to help you? I don't know how to create presentations, but you could forward your phone calls to me, and I could take down your boss's messages...and schedule meetings too, if you tell me what days are best."

Peggy stared at me, wide-eyed.

I thought perhaps I had stepped on her toes and given her the impression I didn't think she could do it all on her own. Though I could totally see that she *could*. But I was bored, and she had so many tasks going at once, she looked like a super-efficient office octopus. Helping was a win-win.

"That would be *amazing*," she said. "Are you sure?"

The way she said it clued me in on two valuable pieces of information. One, it must not be common in business for people to offer to help with other people's work. Two, even though I'd worried whether Peggy would like me since my personality was the complete opposite of hers, I'd just made my first friend.

That week, I found out that Peggy always had the most work because she assisted the new up-and-coming marketing manager. He was a fairly new hire and looking to climb the corporate ladder in record time, so he seemed to do the work of two or three people, which meant he needed the same from his assistant.

Though I never asked much about it because I knew from Aunt Sue to stay away from office gossip (in addition to avoiding calling her Aunt Sue at the office), I gathered that for some reason, Rhonda had never offered to help Peggy. Also, they couldn't hire another assistant to share the workload.

Peggy said that having me there was almost like being on vacation.

I picked up any extra task that usually piled up for her and that didn't take any special skills. I did the filing, answering phones, scheduling meetings, and picking up presentations at the printers, which allowed her to focus on the work she loved and was really good at.

Guess what? Peggy *did* talk, especially now that she had more time. I picked up some really valuable computer skills from her and learned a lot about the company the few times she was able to go out to lunch with me, which she said she had never gotten to do before.

So far, I was loving my experience in the business world. But I was also worried. I knew that if Marketing could hire a second assistant for the manager, I'd be a shoo-in, but that wasn't possible. I only had one week left to earn a place, and I wasn't sure how I was going to go about it.

I shared my goal and my fears with Peggy. She listened quietly and then told me she would give it some thought and let me know if she had any ideas.

That was one of the things I loved about Peggy. Where I would have burst out with any and all ideas I had right off the top of my head, she would marinate instead. She only gave me her very best ideas.

When it was already late Friday morning and she hadn't shared anything with me, I thought perhaps she hadn't had any ideas. Then Peggy surprised me by asking if I had an hour to spare for a field trip.

"Sure!" I said, excited at the idea.

Peggy smiled and took me on a tour of the rest of the company. We stopped in each department and spoke with the assistants there.

"This is April," she told each of them by way of introduction. "I mentioned her in my memo." Each time, I beamed, said hello, and thrust out my friendly, confident handshake. Each assistant shook my hand and said they thought what I was doing was fantastic and they were so grateful for the help. Then they each handed me a list of tasks they needed help with and the best days for me to do so.

I was excited just to meet new people and to know I had work to do for the following week.

Then Peggy shared the true brilliance of her idea: "Pretty much every assistant in the departments that are doing well is overworked. They all need help, but tend not to complain or ask for it—just like you saw with me. Some of those departments probably do have the budget to hire someone new, and I thought doing this would give you the opportunity to show them just how great of a helper you are."

I was speechless. (And for me, that says a lot!) Professional or not, I threw my arms around Peggy and gave her the biggest hug.

"This is the best idea possible! Thank you so, so much!" I was so excited but also a little sad. I loved working with Peggy and hated the thought of leaving her.

But then she said, "I don't want you to leave Marketing, but if you have to, I wanted to do whatever I could to make sure you're just down the hall somewhere."

"You've given me a great opportunity, and I'll turn it into something amazing!" I said, with all the optimism and confidence that had gotten me this far.

Monday of the next week started my round-robin of helping in any department that needed me. I had a hodgepodge of tasks from each assistant. They ranged from easy, quick, and fun to hard, lengthy, and monotonous.

Some of the tasks required skills I didn't even possess, which made me wonder just what was in that memo Peggy had sent. One of those came from an assistant named Janice, a fiery redhead in her mid-fifties who worked for a department head, Mr. Landau. He was known as the meanest guy in the office. I had yet to meet him, but I had heard a lot.

She handed me about twenty-five typed sheets of paper. Each page had so many handwritten notes and changes in red, it looked like the paper would either bleed to death or be given an F.

"I'm so glad you're young and good with computers, April," Janice said. "I haven't learned them yet, and Mr. Landau wants this entire white paper typed up and formatted on the computer so we can update it easily whenever we need to. Can you do that by the end of the day?"

"Absolutely!" I said, crossing my fingers that formatting this document on the company computer would work like formatting my school newspaper, since I knew I could do that for sure.

Right at that moment, Mr. Landau walked into Janice's office. Mr. Meanest-in-the-Office himself. He did look stern and tough, but all he said was, "So this is the kid who can make my vital project happen today?" in a voice that would have made him a great mob boss.

"Sure is," Janice replied. "And thank goodness, because I already told you I can't do it."

"Humph," he grunted, looking at both of us and then walking back to his office.

Now I know what you're thinking: *April, why did you lie?*

Valid question.

Candidly, I didn't think I was lying. Sure, I'd never done it before and I didn't know how. However, it never occurred to me that meant I couldn't do it. I always assumed I could.

Janice set me up in a vacant office and I got to work. The typing part was easy. That only took me about three hours. It also helped me realize that the only time I could type 120 words per minute was in typing class. But I was still pretty fast.

I took lunch to celebrate and figured I'd be done early, since all I had to do was format it when I got back. As I ate, I congratulated myself for doing such a great job. It was only Wednesday and I'd helped four departments already! I had also gotten rave reviews from the assistants. Surely one of the departments would want to keep me.

Now finishing this "big, important project" for Mr. Landau early would be hitting it out of the park.

I got back to the office and sat down, ready to conquer formatting. Then I noticed I had accidentally set a stapler down on the keyboard's Return key before I'd left. And now all but the final paragraph of my twenty-five typed pages were nowhere to be seen.

I panicked. Were they gone?

As I felt heat rise from my stomach to my chest and face, I realized the screen was still moving. I picked the stapler up, and that's when I noticed the document was on page 1,256.

Okay. The good news was my twenty-five typed pages were probably still there. The bad news was that it took significantly longer to delete each line than it had to add all those blank lines in the first place. I was really worried that I wouldn't finish on time.

But I just knew I could do this. I was too scared to ask anyone for help. So I held my finger on that Delete button and prayed for it to speed up and get back to my typed pages. Save me, Delete button!

By 4 p.m., I wasn't even halfway back to my original twenty-five pages.

My eyes welled up with tears. I didn't think I was going to make it. I'd have to tell the meanest man in the office that I really couldn't do what I had said I could. I'd probably be fired.

As the first tear slid down my cheek, a man who helped run the Synthetic Industries factory popped into the vacant office with a grin. His name was Preston.

"Hey, April! I just heard from your mom you're doing work in the office. I didn't realize they put you in my office for the afternoon."

I hastily wiped the tear off of my cheek and tried to look normal.

"Hi, Preston," I stammered, hoping to distract him from my red face. "This is your office? I thought you worked in the factory."

He nodded. "I do both—office work and managing the factory hands-on. Jack of all trades and all that." He paused and added, "I was about to ask you how it was going, but I think I can see it's not going as well as you'd like. What happened?"

I spilled my whole sordid tale.

Normally, I'd have been embarrassed to tell Preston about all these mistakes. He was one of the youngest people at Synthetic Industries. I guessed he was in his late twenties and thought he was really handsome. Every time my mom had introduced me to him, I felt like my face was on fire.

However, desperation has a way of wiping away your pride.

Luckily, Preston had the answer. "I'm gonna help you out, kid. There's a magic button that will fix this," he said with a grin.

He walked over to the keyboard and highlighted my one lonely paragraph and cut it. Then he reached over and hit a key on the far right of my keyboard I hadn't paid any attention to. It was the Home key.

It really was like magic. Immediately, I was at the first page of my white paper. Then he hit Page Down twenty-four times rapidly and placed my last paragraph at the end.

I was too relieved to be mortified that I'd had no idea these keys existed or what they did.

As I was about to breathe the world's largest sigh of relief, Preston said, "I can show you what you need to know to format this document, and teaching you will only take about twenty minutes. You won't be finished by five o'clock though."

Then he said, "I think you should tell Mr. Landau what happened and that you're going to be late, then come back here and I'll show you. Everybody makes mistakes, April. I've made a ton. Owning up to them and sharing your plan to fix them isn't just what's right, it's also something that will make you stand out because a lot of people aren't brave enough to do it."

I took in a huge shoulder-moving breath. "Okay, I will." I left his office and walked over to Mr. Landau's department like I was walking the plank.

I knocked on the office door with more confidence than I felt and heard him say, "Come in."

I walked in and took a big gulp before starting my explanation. He cut me off with a mischievous look in his eyes. "Well, kid, are you here to hand in my project early?"

"No, sir," I said with all the disappointment I felt in myself.

I went on to explain the whole situation honestly—my overconfidence, my mistake, Preston's help, and that I'd miss the deadline I'd committed to. I added that I'd work overtime without pay to make it right and not go home until it was done.

His expression was unreadable. Then he opened his mouth and started cackling. He laughed long and hard while I stared at him wide-eyed and worried.

"Kid, that took serious balls. You're going to do okay. In fact, I may just end up working for you!"

I was shocked. I thanked him then ran out of his office and back to Preston's to thank him and learn how to finish formatting the white paper. I delivered it to Mr. Landau's office at 6:15 p.m., after he'd gone home.

I'll never know for sure, but I think Preston may have given Mr. Landau a heads-up and asked him to go easy on me. I also think Mr. Landau's reputation as a meanie was based on an act that he had fun with.

I walked to my car thinking I'd learned a very valuable lesson that day. I promised myself I'd put it into action immediately.

The next morning, Janet, head of the International Shipping department, met me at the door when I came into the office. She said the international sales assistant had transferred to her department and was in training all that day and Friday. In the meantime, her former boss was traveling overseas and didn't have anyone to help him. She needed someone to retrieve faxes from the assistant's old computer and read them to the international sales manager over the phone. Could I do it?

This was my chance to apply what I'd learned. I had no idea how to retrieve faxes from a computer, but I said, "Absolutely!"

Wait…you thought I'd tell her no and turn down the job? Nah.

The lesson I learned was to speak up quickly, own my mistakes, and offer a solution. I still thought that if it seemed like I could figure it out, I should just say yes!

I was a little familiar with the International Sales department. I had previously helped the sales assistant Janet spoke of earlier in the week. She needed me to catch up on about two months of overdue customer filing. I remembered her telling me her job was way too big for one person and how excited she was to transfer to a new department.

Silently wishing I'd paid more attention as she retrieved and printed the faxes for her manager, Ron, I turned on her computer and set about figuring out how to get them.

Luck was on my side. It was easy! I got all the faxes and printed them out in less than ten minutes. Now I had to get them to Ron.

Janet may have meant for me to give them to her, but I knew Ron was in Europe and six hours ahead of me. That meant he'd only have two hours to decide how to answer these faxes and get back to the clients before their business day was over.

I dialed the last number Pat had posted for Ron's hotel (being sure to add a one + the international country code). He picked up immediately.

"Hello. Ron Sutton here."

He had the *best* British accent, and I couldn't help but smile.

"Hi, Ron. I'm April. Janet asked me to help you with your faxes this morning. I've printed them out, and I can read them to you. If you tell me how you want to reply, I'll make sure they go out within the hour so you can catch everyone."

This was the part I loved! Helping people and making a difference under tight deadlines.

"Splendid, Ayyyypril!"

He jumped right in and I took down all the information then spent the next hour replying with his responses and faxing them back out.

When Janet finally had a free moment, she rushed into the office. "April, were you able to get the faxes out? It's getting late overseas and we need to get them to Ron."

"Yes ma'am, I did. I also called and spoke with Ron, got the responses and quotes for the orders, and sent them back to the clients," I said with pride.

She stood there shocked.

I was so excited. Besides Aunt Sue, Janet was the only other female leader in the company, and I was really proud that she had gotten to see me at my best.

"That's fantastic, April! Would you mind staying here today and tomorrow to help with incoming faxes? Ron hasn't had time to hire anyone to replace Pat, and he's not back in the US for another two weeks."

"I would love to!"

I was certain I'd just found my opportunity.

Ron needed help, and I could help him.

I spent the rest of the day gathering all the information I would need for our call Friday morning. It was my last official day. I hoped it would also be the day they asked me to stay!

The next morning, I called Ron, just as I had the day before. I updated him on all the correspondence, got his answers, and took care of the customers.

Near the end of the call, he said, "I must say, April, I like your proactive approach. I usually call Pat there in the office, but sometimes she misses my call, and we play a game of phone tag for hours. I appreciate you phoning me straightaway when you get into the office."

"I'm happy to, Ron," I said. "I have one other item if you have a moment?"

"Sure, sure."

"I'm a temporary employee, and I've been floating around for the past two weeks. Today is my last day. However, if you'd like more help, I am available. You just have to let Sue Harper in Human Resources know."

Ron said, "That's a splendid idea! I'll phone her immediately."

Ron and I continued to work together, sight unseen, for two weeks before he got back to the states. If he was surprised I was just sixteen, he didn't say.

He asked me to stay on full-time until school started back. By then, he'd hired and I'd help train an amazing woman named

Bea for the full-time assistant role. They both asked me to stay and work from noon to 6 p.m. during my senior year as part of my school's co-op program.

I learned so much about sales, service, and friendship during my time working with Ron and Bea and the rest of the office staff at Synthetic Industries. That role and those people had a huge impact on my life—I will always be grateful to all of them for taking a chance on an unknown kid.

My Advice

Don't worry if there isn't a place for you where you'd most like to be. You have the power and the ability to create one.

As you know, I didn't really have all the skills or qualifications I'd needed to work at Synthetic Industries, but the belief that *I could figure it out* led me to both opportunities and people who could help.

The same is true for you.

Chapter Five

GETTIN' OUT OF DODGE

As much as I loved business, I felt deep in my bones that I was destined to be on television.

At the time, I thought it was perfect for me. TV is Glamorous and Special, which would make *me* Glamorous and Special too.

When I was really young, I watched the famous TV anchor Barbara Walters with immense admiration. My mom would tell me, "If you work really hard and go to college, you could be the next Barbara Walters." But to me, that sounded like: "If you become a television newscaster like her, you will be loved."

It would certainly explain my obsession with it.

I had no question I was bound for television and college, though I knew I'd have to find a way to pay for the latter. The good news was I believed I was exceptionally smart, and I had full faith that the college of my choice would happily give me a scholarship in return for my attendance at their school.

Then of course they would be able to tell people I had gone to school there after I became a Big TV Star. (I cringe writing those words now, but they are embarrassingly true.)

So as other kids were trying to figure out which college would be most fun or had their particular major, while factoring in how much their parents could afford to pay, I was searching for schools responsible for the people who were delivering me the news.

I don't remember how I narrowed it down, but at one point it was between Northwestern and Boston University. BU won hands down for two reasons.

One, they had a former executive producer from ABC News (Barbara's network!) as a professor, who would undoubtedly give me all the secrets of getting hired and groom me to take over the airwaves.

Two, it was farther away from home than Northwestern, and getting as far away as possible was crucial to me.

I checked the standardized test score requirements and briefly spent time convincing myself that though I absolutely hated cold and rain, it wouldn't be *that* bad for four years. I also talked on the phone for about ten minutes to a BU student who said it was awesome.

That was enough for me to decide that I would not only apply to Boston University but also do so under early decision, just as my senior year of high school started, which meant I agreed not to apply to any other school.

All the eggs—one basket!

This seemed completely reasonable to me. I thought Boston University was the best school for me, I was smart, I was destined to go there, so let's get this paperwork out of the way and make it happen.

I also applied for both a scholarship and financial aid. I was pretty sure that I would get a scholarship, but my counselor—who was excited that I was applying to schools so early but not aware that I was only applying to just one—said I would absolutely qualify for financial aid based on my mom's income, so I should do that too.

Selection to Boston University was really competitive, especially for the broadcasting school, but I wasn't worried. I had a single-minded determination and truly believed my dreams would come true.

Here's the crazy part: in a way, they did.

BU accepted less than twenty percent of all applicants, and even fewer applicants under early decision. For months, I endured family and friends telling me how unlikely it was for me to get chosen and how foolish it was for me to think I would. I alternated between the invigorating burn in my stomach of *I'll show them* and the fear that they were right and I'd look stupid for thinking I was special.

I waited in those tense months much like a duck moving full speed across a pond. To others, I looked cool and calm, moving effortlessly across the water with no worries. Underneath, my mind, like a duck's little legs, moved a hundred miles per hour, constantly wondering when that letter would arrive.

The day it came, the single, regular-sized envelope was the only item in the mail. I opened the mailbox, gasped, and slammed it shut. I tried to remember whether the envelope size indicated anything. My stomach dropped with this thought: *Wasn't a small envelope a "Thanks but no thanks" and a big envelope a "Welcome! Here's all you need to know"?*

Then as quickly as my spirits fell, they lifted. Early decision— it would be a small envelope either way. There was plenty of time for information packets later if it was a yes.

I silently thanked God I was alone that afternoon. If it was bad news, I'd have time to compose myself before I told anyone else. If it was good news, I'd have all afternoon to savor the sweet victory before my mom started peppering me with "But have you thought of this and this?" questions that reflected her worry that good things didn't happen to people like us.

I snatched the envelope out of the mailbox and tore it open like there was a million-dollar check inside. There wasn't. Instead, I read a few lines of text starting with "We are excited to inform you that you've been accepted to Boston University under our early decision program…"

I don't think anyone could have convinced me to trade that validation for the million-dollar check.

I told everyone who would listen—teachers, my coworkers at Synthetic Industries, my family, anyone.

On the flip side, I listened to absolutely no one when they asked about tuition or whether I had concerns about getting a full scholarship. That included my guidance counselor. After hearing I was going to accept my admission to BU, she reminded me that I had been offered a full ride to the University of Tennessee at Chattanooga. I only had to accept it.

I don't think I *physically* thumbed my nose at her or at any local school, but it was pretty close.

The day the financial letter came from BU, I tore it open and began to read about my package. It started with a sentence mentioning a "historically competitive environment" and numerous "highly qualified candidates" and then went on to list the amount of scholarship money they were offering me.

My eyes bugged out.

My breath came in and out way too quickly.

I did the math. My scholarship and financial aid *together* would be about $10,000 a year. The tuition was $28,000 a year.

Before room and board.

Or books.

Or food.

Tuition alone with the scholarship and aid was more than twice all the money I made in a year at Synthetic Industries.

I stared at that treacherous letter that basically stated: "You're smart, April, but *not smart enough*." My stomach felt like it was full of lead weights and heat rose up my body into my neck and face as a feeling of intense shame, strong and suffocating, washed over me and took hold.

I assumed the scholarship recipients were all valedictorians with 4.0 GPAs instead of my 3.9. I imagined them celebrating their success with their normal families.

Then my ego, ever my defender, reminded me that the people who got scholarships didn't need to work thirty hours a week while going to high school to help support themselves and their families.

I cycled through an array of emotions—feeling sorry for myself, then berating myself for not being better so this whole situation went differently, and finally to complete and utter shock.

This had not gone as planned.

I sat on that letter, the shame, and the disappointment for several days. Finally, I told my mom. I remember a lecture on "eggs in one basket" and "thinking I was too good for Tennessee."

Mostly, I remember thinking that whatever I would do would be up to me. I was scrambling to find a Plan B.

I had until January to let BU know whether I would be attending, and I waited until the last day to let them know I wouldn't. I kept hoping somehow it would work out, but it didn't.

It was a crushing blow.

I felt like I had *just missed* my dream.

I was in a daze for a couple of months, wondering what I was supposed to do with my life. It was the first time a plan I'd made simply didn't happen. I had never imagined that being an outcome I'd face. Somehow I had thought I could achieve anything I wanted sheerly by wanting it badly enough and being able to put in the work.

The one thought that didn't occur to me at the time was that sometimes what seems like a disaster is actually leading you to something so much better.

Without that knowledge, I trudged on.

In the early spring of my senior year, I did the only thing I could think of. My mom was pressuring me to take the full ride to the local university and live at home, so I applied to the University of Tennessee in Knoxville. They had a good broadcasting program. Not BU level, but good. And they were two hours away. Distance was still more important to me than free. I explained to any interested parties that Boston University was just too expensive, so I'd be going to UTK.

The tuition, food, room, and board expenses at UTK were a little under $6,000 a year, and I hoped this time the scholarship gods would be on my side.

I applied later in the year than most other students but was still accepted. Big sigh of relief! However, there were no more scholarships, there was no more housing, and the financial aid I'd previously applied for had all been claimed. Attending UTK would now cost around $7,000 a year. While that was way more within reach than BU had been, I still didn't know how I could pay for it.

It's relevant to note two points here.

One, I had a big fear of college debt because it seemed like such a large amount of money to owe before you knew what kind of job you were getting or what it would pay.

Two, I didn't have anyone to cosign a loan for me. My mother and all of the men in her life (my stepfather having made an exit) had terrible credit.

I hadn't always known that. I knew she didn't have credit cards or car loans, but I never gave a lot of thought as to why. I learned that lesson in the fall of my senior year when I wanted to buy a nicer car than the one I'd purchased from her. My main goal at the time was to have windows that could roll up and down (ah, the quirks of the first car) and an air conditioner that worked. At seventeen, you have to have a cosigner for a loan, even if you made enough to pay the car payment, which I did. I asked my mom if she could cosign, and she said yes.

We went to the dealer, found what I considered to be an amazing car (the windows and AC worked and it was within my budget) and applied for the loan. At the time, I knew nothing about credit scores or how they worked. All I knew was that I had a job and made more money than most kids my age, and that I'd always paid my bills on time. (See Avon Invoice in Chapter 3.)

The car salesperson, learning I was just seventeen and had no credit history (I didn't realize my payments to Avon wouldn't count), said he'd only be pulling my mother's credit for the loan. I never understood why my mom agreed to have her credit report pulled. Surely she knew what was on there.

After seeing her score, the salesperson unceremoniously escorted us out of the building, muttering under his breath that he'd never seen such a terrible credit score and that we didn't belong there.

I. Was. Mortified.

Trying to hold back tears, I felt the heat of shame wash over me and turn my face red, followed quickly by outrage at my mother for letting it happen. I couldn't look at her as we drove home in silence.

Growing up, even when I was working, I always felt intimidated in nice stores and worried they'd somehow know I was poor and ask me to leave. That never happened, but this was a bigger version of that nightmare coming true right before my eyes.

(Decades later, having found financial success and sporting a credit score of nearly 850, I *still* get slightly nervous when anyone wants to check my credit report. I think that's a part of why I prefer to just pay in full.)

So just a few weeks before high school graduation, I was still trying to figure out how I would pay for college. I couldn't talk to my mom about it because I knew it was my responsibility. I didn't discuss money with my friends because I was ashamed. And I didn't feel like I could ask anyone else in my family for advice.

Interestingly, I didn't reach out to Aunt Sue for her thoughts either. I was on the precipice of being an adult, and I thought that meant you took care of your challenges all on your own.

I continued to tell people at school and at Synthetic Industries that I was going to UTK the following fall. One day, I received faxed letters from customers all over the world wishing "Mr. April" a wonderful college experience at UTK. (Because we had only spoken over fax, and many of our international customers assumed I was a man.)

For the first time in my life, I didn't have a plan. I had no idea what I was going to do, and I was too ashamed to tell anyone the truth about it. I felt like I'd failed and that none of my dreams were going to come true. I kept up a good attitude, but I was really struggling. I had accepted that I wasn't going to college that fall, but I couldn't face letting anyone know I'd failed. Only my mother and close family knew.

At the end of August, the folks at Synthetic Industries took me out for a celebratory lunch and gave me a cake.

Meanwhile, I interviewed for other jobs and privately told Aunt Sue that I needed another year to work and save up for school. I asked her not to share that information since everyone at work was so excited I was going to college. She agreed to keep my secret, though she also told me there was no reason to hide my change of plans or to be embarrassed. She said there were *many paths*, not just one right path, to the career I wanted.

Thanks to learning about several temporary agencies through my work at Synthetic Industries, it was easy to find a new role. I'd developed a lot of marketable skills over the year. Plus I'd been in the corporate world, and my salary needs were still low compared to others with my level of experience.

I chose a role at a young company run by a dynamic woman in her early thirties. I would be her research assistant and one of her first employees as she moved her business out of her home and into a cool designer office in downtown Chattanooga.

Her name was Merri Mai. Though her name sounded old-school Southern, she was the most cosmopolitan woman I'd ever met. She was great at business and an amazingly hard worker, and I learned skills from her I still continue to use today.

She'd been a human resources assistant at a light industrial firm, where she developed an in-house screening process to ensure the best recruiting for her company. Within a year, the company had decreased its attrition rate by fifty percent, and other local companies started asking her to help them with their hiring process. She had started helping them part-time and eventually ran the business full-time, just two years before hiring me.

By that time, Merri Mai was a licensed private investigator who did background checks and employment screening for well-known national companies. She also did competitive analysis and other services, all of which I learned to do while working for her.

When I started, the plan was for me to get my PI license as soon as I was twenty-one and continue to grow with the business. She gave me opportunities to network and speak in front of large groups to market the company, and that really built my confidence and taught me vital skills for business and life. In return, I worked tirelessly and learned as much as possible while constantly pushing myself to exceed her high expectations.

Merri Mai never asked me to do work she wouldn't do or hadn't already done. While I worked for her, I grew by leaps and bounds. It was an excellent education in entrepreneurialism and gave me another view of life.

She hadn't finished college but was still successful, well-respected in the community, and someone I looked up to very much. She also taught me the importance of personal and business credit. One of the services we provided in our employment screening was credit checks. I learned so much about how to make sure my own credit report was pristine.

My credit history started when I bought a bedroom set. Furniture stores are much more likely than auto dealers or mortgage companies to extend credit to someone without one, as long as they have a good employment history. I paid a *terrible* interest rate (I think it was eighteen or twenty percent), but it was worth it to establish a credit history. I happily paid it each month, determined to never have another experience like I had at the car dealership.

Merri Mai also told me something I still tell clients today: banks usually only give you money when you *don't need it*, so get a line of credit for your business early, even if you don't have an immediate need.

I was continuing to grow in my business knowledge, as a person and as Merri Mai's right hand. I'd even moved out of my mother's house and got an apartment with my best friend. My life was definitely moving forward.

Still I was restless and felt like something was missing. Even as I saw lots of folks around me succeeding without a college degree, I still couldn't shake the feeling that even if it took me ten years going to school at night, I needed to complete that goal for myself.

That spring, I enrolled in college at the University of Tennessee at Chattanooga, taking one night class that semester.

Yes, the same one that had offered me a full ride just a year before.

Yes, the one that I had thumbed my nose up at.

Yes, I paid full-price tuition to attend.

It was both humbling and a fantastic lesson.

And as it turned out, taking that class changed the entire course of my life.

It was English composition (the first of a basic list of requirements for any degree) and I enjoyed it a lot. Because it was night school, there were a lot of other businesspeople and adults, and not as many students that were my age. That suited me just fine. I always felt like I fit in with adults more than people my age anyway.

I met a man in his mid-twenties named Chris who was finishing his requirements for an undergraduate degree in accounting. Typical of a math-loving person, he had waited as long as possible to do any writing requirements. I was the opposite; I would procrastinate on math courses as long as I could!

I helped him a lot in our class and got to know him. He'd been in the Air Force, and now he was in college to finish his degree.

One night, I overheard Chris say, "I'm really glad the Air Force is paying for this English class even after they let me take all those other courses while I was serving." He laughed. "I'm terrible at this, so I might have to take it twice!"

I swung my head around so fast I should've gotten whiplash. "What did you say?"

"That I'm glad this is on the Air Force's dime."

"Right. The military gives you money for college after you serve for four years—I knew that. But what were you saying about going to school while you were in the Air Force?" I leaned forward.

"Oh, the Air Force lets you go to school while you're in too. They actually pay seventy-five percent of the tuition, and you just pay twenty-five percent of that and buy your books."

"And you still get other money too?"

Chris nodded. "Yes, from the GI Bill. You invest $1,200 during your first year, and they'll give you $30,000 for college or training after a waiting period."

I stared at him in disbelief.

He continued, "You can start using that after just two years in. I used the tuition assistance program while I was in, because paying just twenty-five percent of tuition was cheap, and then I could use my GI Bill for a master's degree later."

At this point, I was really interested.

Why had I blown off all of those recruiters who had called my house after I took the military entrance exam in high school? (I had no interest in the military at the time, but if you took the test, you got extra credit.) I never even listened to what they were offering when they called because I considered myself way too girly for the military and much more college material.

Maybe I had been too quick to judge.

Now our instructor was talking, so I leaned forward even more and whispered, "So you want to be a CPA and they let you do accounting? Do they let anyone do what they want for work?"

"Sort of," Chris hedged. "You can get a guaranteed job if your entrance exam scores are high enough. As long as you graduate from the training course for that job, you're in. If you don't graduate, you can take another job that the Air Force picks for you, or you have the right to go home."

I was starting to imagine myself in ugly military-green outfits. "Do they have broadcasters. Like, not just on radio but on TV?"

"Oh yeah. But they all have to live overseas. That's the only place they need them."

Wait. A. Minute.

The military would let me have my dream job right now, pay me to do it, allow me to attend college at a reduced price, and give me more financial aid on top of that?

I stood up. The teacher looked at me in surprise.

I said, "I'm sorry, I just realized I have to be somewhere," grabbed my books and bag, and ran out of the classroom. My grand exit was a little anticlimactic because the recruiting office in my town had closed for the night. I would have to try again the next day.

I went back to the college library to research military broadcasters. My knowledge was limited to Robin Williams as Adrian Cronauer in *Good Morning, Vietnam*. I found out the military would train me for both TV and radio. And that the training was considered better than what I would get in a four-year college program. There were lots of former military broadcasters working in the media. Pat Sajak was one! Well he hosted *Wheel of Fortune*, not the news, but that seemed like a great gig.

I was about to come out of my skin and could barely sleep that night. I hadn't told anyone. Not my mom, not my best friend, no one. I thought they'd think I was crazy. I figured it was better to tell them once it was done.

The next day, I showed up to the recruiting office and shared that I wanted to join so I could be a television broadcaster and that I needed to know the process—specifically, how long it would take and what they needed from me so I could start immediately.

The recruiter, wearing a nametag that read "Hartburg," simply stared at me. (He later told me that a nearly six-foot blonde, which I was in heels, walking into the recruiting office in a suit on a Saturday giving him instructions wasn't a normal occurrence.)

Once he realized I was indeed in the right place, Sergeant Hartburg began scheduling me for the military entrance exam.

I closed one eye, thinking back. "My English teacher gave us extra credit if we took that test my junior year when the recruiter guy came. I don't remember my score, but lots of recruiters called for months afterwards."

Again, Sergeant Hartburg's eyes widened. Then he turned to his computer and looked up my test scores. "Okay, wow. Your scores are higher than about ninety-eight percent of military recruits. You can do any job we have!"

"Great!" I exhaled. "I want to be a broadcaster."

He wrinkled his noise like a kid being offered broccoli instead of cookies. "Broadcasting only requires a score of sixty-nine. You're in the high nineties. You could go to the Air Force

Academy free for four years, get your degree, then serve four years afterwards as an officer and get paid way more."

"And then I'd be a broadcaster and an officer?"

"Well no...only enlisted airmen can be broadcasters. It's a really small career field. Over three hundred and fifty thousand people are in the Air Force, but only about three hundred of them are broadcasters. That's less than one percent. You have to audition to even go to the training, and they don't select a lot of people for that either. So few, actually, that I've never known anyone who did it."

Every comment Sergeant Hartburg made to dissuade me from broadcasting made it sound more special. Plus, TV stations considered the military's broadcast training program better than a four-year degree program from any college because it was hands-on.

I realized Sergeant Hartburg was still talking and tried to catch enough context clues to understand what I'd missed.

"...and the thing about OSI, April, is that you could leave there and go straight into the FBI. And they give you a sign-on bonus, which broadcasting doesn't."

"Wait...OSI, like investigating?" I wrinkled my nose.

"Yeah. You work for an investigator now, so it makes sense. And you have to have high scores, which you do. Plus there's that cash sign-on bonus." His eyes lit up as he finished with a big don't-you-want-this-shiny-new-car smile.

We could have wasted a lot of time going back and forth. He didn't seem to understand my mind was made up.

I grabbed a Sharpie off his desk, opened up my padfolio, and wrote in big capital letters "BROADCASTING OR BUST." Then I tore off the page, held it up, and smiled.

Hartburg held up his hands. "Okay, okay. I'll figure out how to set up the audition and call you Monday."

"Perfect!" I grinned, feeling an exhilaration that filled me with energy and hope. I floated to my car, turned the radio on full blast, and yelled the lyrics at the top of my lungs.

As I caught my breath, I realized I'd just made a life-changing decision, and I had to tell everyone. My best friend would be excited for me. My mom would hate it because I was going so far away, so I'd tell her last.

Then my heart sank…Merri Mai. I idolized her, but I didn't want her life; I wanted my own dream. I was terrified to tell her that. I didn't want to hurt her. I didn't want to disappoint her either. I wrestled with how to tell her for the rest of the day. Some people would have procrastinated, put it off, or even waited to see the results of the broadcasting audition, but I couldn't do that. My gut was all twisted up every time I thought of it, and not telling her right away would feel like lying.

I called her that evening and asked if I could come by Sunday afternoon to talk about something important. It felt like a breakup. I also had doubts.

Was I making a mistake?

Was this foolish?

What if I hated the military?

What if they hated *me*?

What if I never found another boss like Merri Mai?

What I couldn't ignore though was that *deep-down feeling* that this was what I was supposed to do. The feeling was stronger than any doubt. It made me feel a combination of excited and terrified that I'd never felt before. It was too compelling to ignore.

I grabbed several school yearbooks with pictures of me at different ages. All the yearbooks had features about how I wanted to be a TV news anchor on some page or another. I took them with me to Merri Mai's house.

The yearbooks were my proof that this dream had been in place long before I had started working for her. I felt like I needed that proof. I'd never told her about it because I was ashamed that I'd failed what I felt was the first step to get there—going to a great college.

The conversation didn't go well.

Merri Mai was more reserved than normal and asked only a few questions. She seemed confused when I confirmed that I was happy in my role at her company, had learned a lot, and felt appreciated.

Seeing her bewildered look, I began to explain, showing her yearbook pictures and stumbling on my words. I spoke around the lump in my throat, tears flowing down my cheeks. "It's been amazing working for you. I've learned so much and I can never thank you enough. But the thing is, I've wanted this forever, and if I don't go after this dream, I'll never forgive myself. I'm young, and I've already made mistakes, but mistakes I can learn from. I won't grow or learn from regrets."

When I finished explaining, I saw only disappointment on her face. I offered to continue to work for her and train my replacement until I went to basic training, but she said two weeks' notice was all she needed from me.

What I desperately needed to hear was, "I hate to lose you, but I'm even more excited about what's next for you!" But those words never came. We briefly talked about wrapping up my projects, and I left, deflated.

It was the only time I saw Merri Mai stumble as a leader. Like all of her shining moments, that misstep taught me an immense lesson. Driving home, I committed to always value people's growth and dreams more than what they did for my team or my company. I wanted to be the person who would share in someone's excitement in moving toward their goals.

The next few weeks were a blur of wrapping up work projects, doing a broadcasting voice audition for my Air Force recruiter, and finding new work as a temporary employee. The good news was that my work for Merri Mai had allowed me to develop relationships with some really prominent temporary agencies, so it was easy to get a great assignment quickly. My position at the Air Pollution Control Bureau would keep me busy until I left for basic training. I even got a salary increase.

Once my voice audition tape was sent out, it was a waiting game. The recruiter estimated it would take six weeks to hear back. If I passed, he would find out when I was scheduled for the dreaded basic training based on when I needed to be finished and ready to attend what the Air Force referred to as "technical training school." In my case, it would be the Basic Broadcaster Course.

While I waited, I hired a personal trainer to help me get in shape. I knew I needed to be stronger and able to run at least a couple of miles. Also, I couldn't do a single push-up.

Five weeks later, I came home to a message on my answering machine from my recruiter. He told me to call the office, and I just knew we'd gotten audition results early. I could barely contain my excitement.

He answered on the first ring.

I chirped, "Hey there! It's April! What's up?"

Speaking in the kindest voice I'd ever heard from him, he said, "April, I'm so sorry. You failed the voice audition. I have the paper here and you can come see their feedback, or I can read it to you over the phone."

Sergeant Hartburg kept talking, but his voice started to sound like the teacher in the Peanuts cartoons: "Waaa, wa waaa wa, waaaaa, wa wa waaaaa…"

I leaned back against the wall in our little apartment kitchen and slid down it until I hit the floor with a thud. I sat there mute, staring out the window as tears fell unchecked down my cheeks. A monumental feeling of failure washed over me. At some point, I squeaked out, "Thank you. I'll call you back," and hung up. But I didn't move from my place on the floor.

I sat there for hours, unmoving, torturing myself with thoughts. What a big mistake I had just made. All the eggs in one basket again. What had I done?

No Air Force.

No college.

No career.

How could I have messed up again so soon in such a big way?

This was *not* me.

Unless it was. Was I a loser?

Was failing my *new thing*?

Is this why no one in my family had pursued their dreams? Because it never worked out?

When my best friend got home, she found me there on the kitchen floor. Over the next couple of weeks, she and everyone who cared about me did everything they could think of to help me deal with the news. They said…

"You can do lots of great work in the Air Force besides broadcasting."

"April, you can do anything. Audition again!"

"You're going to be successful no matter what."

None of it resonated with me. I was in a tailspin. For the first time in my life, I was unable to reframe the situation, find a solution, or believe that it would work out.

One day, I came home after work and heard my recruiter's voice on the answering machine again. I half ignored him because I assumed it was another pitch for going into the Air Force anyway and being an OSI investigator. Then I heard him say, "Another recruit could really use your help. He wants to go into broadcasting and is really nervous about the audition. Would you talk to him?"

Some people might say this was more salt in the wound than a gift, but it gave me the opportunity to focus on someone outside myself instead of my failure. I let him know I'd love to help.

The next day, I jumped on the phone with the other recruit. I got the awkward part out of the way immediately.

"So, Brian, I should tell you that I failed my audition, because my vocal resonance was 'too nasal and tinny.' But I learned everything about the process, all the things you have to send and in what format. I'm happy to help you with yours."

"Wow, that's really cool of you."

"Hey, no biggie." I sounded way more nonchalant than I felt.

I gave him all the information I had about the audition requirements and told him to call me if he had any other questions. Curious, I asked, "Are you nervous about the audition?"

"Nah, I did radio work while I was in high school, and the scripts for the audition are like warm-up vocal exercises we did. I'm pretty confident about my voice. It was the process that worried me. I didn't want to make a mistake on the submission and get disqualified without the instructors even listening. Hartburg said that you submitted a perfect one."

"Well, perfect minus being tinny and nasal." I still felt the sting of those two words that had stolen my dream.

Brian said, "April, I've had vocal training. Your voice isn't nasal or tinny at all."

"You're sweet to say that. Hey, even if my dream isn't coming true, it's pretty cool to help someone else with theirs."

Brian finished his recording and shipped it off in record time. We waited for his audition results together. Of course, I was much more patient to get his back than I had been with my own. Before I knew it, Brian called to thank me for helping him. He'd passed his audition.

I was really happy and excited for him, since he'd gotten what I'd wanted for myself. I felt like that was a big moment for him and for me. Brian thanked me profusely and repeated that he really thought it was worth me auditioning again to see if they had made a mistake on my first one.

For days after the call, his words kept coming back to me: "April, I've had vocal training. Your voice isn't nasal or tinny at all."

Maybe he was just been being nice. I didn't even know what "nasal and tinny" really meant. To me, they meant "bad" and "failed audition," and I hadn't investigated beyond that.

But what if I did? What if I was nervous and my voice sounded weird that day? What if I could get vocal training to fix that? It had to be worth a shot.

I didn't know anyone who did vocal training, but I did know a local news reporter named Tanya. She took tae kwon do with me, and she was really nice. So I asked her if she'd listen to my audition tape and tell me if there were any vocal exercises

I could do to improve, or if she knew of anyone who did vocal training for broadcasters. She said she'd listen to it and get back to me.

I got a call the very next day. The moment I said hello, she asked, "April, where did you record this audition, and what did you use?"

"On a boom box in an empty back office room at the Air Force recruiting station. Why do you ask?"

I could hear the smile in her voice as she said, "Sweetheart, I have the *best* news. I verified with some folks here at the station to be sure. There's *nothing* nasal or tinny about your voice. It was the acoustics in the room! I'm betting it was completely empty with hard floors and just a regular old boom box, right?"

"Yes…" I tried not to get my hopes up, though I was unable to quell my looming excitement.

"That's pretty much the worst place you could've done it because of the echoing, and plus you didn't have a real microphone. I'm ninety-nine percent certain that if we get you into a recording studio, you will ace that audition. And I have a friend who will let you use theirs!"

Tears again, but the best kind. The hopeful, excited, amazing kind you see at the end of a great movie. My heart was soaring, and I couldn't wait to try again.

We recorded my audition in the professional studio and sent off the tape. Five weeks later, I got a call from my recruiter.

I was in!

The feeling was better than any I'd experienced since that first day I had sold Magic Blue Rocks at school and felt my fortunes shifting. This was so much bigger than my dream of broadcasting, or college, or "getting out of Dodge." This was going to change my life.

And it did.

The Air Force gave me so many opportunities. I expected the training, experience, and education, but I got so much more than that. The military completely expanded my worldview—the way I saw people, possibilities, and life in general.

Don't get me wrong, parts were hard as hell. I was terrible at basic training, as I had predicted, but I made it through with sheer grit and tenacity. Also, I didn't do well taking fire while covering stories in war zones! I could act calm in the moment, but for days later I would lose my cookies or go silent.

Having said that, my job was nowhere near as strenuous and dangerous as the roles of so many other servicemembers. It was truly my honor to be able to serve with them. They are real heroes.

While I'm no hero in the military sense, the Air Force did serve as the backdrop for my hero's journey. This one-time "broadcast training reject" overcame and kept going.

After graduating at the top of my broadcast training class, I spent a year in Korea alternating between being a radio DJ and a news reporter and videographer. Then I moved to Germany, where I anchored both radio and television news each day for four years. I earned some of the military's highest broadcasting awards for my work there and while deploying to cover the stories of military members in Bosnia, Kosovo, and Afghanistan. In the time I wasn't broadcasting or working to improve my skills at it, I was going to college to earn a degree in business so that my eggs would *finally* be in diversified baskets!

Those five years of work culminated in the honor of becoming the news anchor and executive producer of the military's largest and most-awarded news program at the time: Air Force Television News. In San Antonio, Texas, I sat at the anchor desk and delivered information to a global audience of seventy-five million people. In the same year, I earned my undergraduate degree in business and started planning what I'd do after the military.

My Advice

I learned more lessons during this particular life experience than any other one I've had.

I feel like, as smart as you are, you've probably been picking out lessons for yourself as you've gone along my journey with me, so I'll just highlight the most important ones.

The first is that it's a gift to have the opportunity to support someone's dreams. Whether we're a leader or a friend, our actions and reactions can encourage and empower. Sometimes it can be challenging to focus on what's best for the other person instead of how we feel, but in my experience, doing so has not only been especially rewarding, it has also usually brought other unexpected opportunities.

I don't think I would have had the courage to investigate my broadcasting audition results without those kind words from Brian—words I would never have heard if I had let my own failure keep me from helping him.

Merri Mai's reaction to me deciding to follow my dream helped me understand how important it is to support employees in their growth, regardless of where that takes them. As a result, past employees have referred other high performers to me, and recruiting great talent has always been easy because they know that *they* matter more than the work they do.

The biggest lesson I took away from this experience is that sometimes the path we have mapped out to find our dreams isn't the best one. There's something better. And that often comes on the heels of what feels like an awful situation or failure. Believing things will work out and having faith that they are happening *for* you and not *to* you will make those opportunities so much easier to see.

It's not always easy to remember that in the exact moment we experience those situations. I sometimes struggle even now. That said, experience has taught me that I'll be extremely grateful for detours and anything that happens differently than I had planned. I simply remind myself that everything holds the possibility of an even better experience than I'd imagined.

I want you to carry that reminder with you too.

I believe in you.

Chapter Six

ATTILA THE HUN

"I want to hire you because you've demonstrated you don't take no for an answer, and I think you'll be great in sales once you learn this business."

The older gentleman was a sales and marketing leader. Sitting across from me, with a poker face, he added, "I just need to be certain you won't run around like Attila the Hun."

I had a vague memory of Attila from school and was sure I wouldn't be as bad as she was.

"I absolutely won't," I responded with confidence.

He nodded.

As soon as the interview ended, I searched online and found that Attila the Hun was actually a man. He was a brilliant military leader who used the strength of his personality to lead others, which I felt was a compliment. But he was also known for brutality, indiscriminate slaughter, and winning at all costs, which I thought was not as complimentary.

But wait, I'm getting ahead of myself.

My career in the Air Force had been amazing. I'd made it to the pinnacle assignment for an Air Force broadcaster—anchoring Air Force Television News—in just five years. I loved every minute of it. I'd graduated college with a bachelor's degree in business and was chomping at the bit for my next mountain to climb.

Unfortunately, as a staff sergeant (E-5) in my late twenties, there was no next mountain for a few years. The next step in my Air Force career would be to run a TV and radio station overseas, but I was considered too young and inexperienced to do it. So I'd have to bide my time and wait until I was promoted to do work I hadn't already done.

A fate worse than death—waiting.

I had felt like I was in a race since I was six years old. A race to have money until money didn't matter. To be successful. To be the person I wanted to be. I ran full-out toward every one of those goals. People and events that slowed me down were a huge frustration or disappointment.

I had what I considered the best job in the world—anchoring the military news to an audience ninety times the size of CNN's (I was always super excited to say that). More notably, I was telling the stories of other military members who were doing the really significant work. I loved it, but it was a "controlled assignment," which meant I could only stay for a limited amount of time. After it was over, I'd be back to doing a job I'd done before but at a TV news station overseas. I wasn't sure how I'd do that. How would I keep from being bored?

I've found that when you really want something, it finds a way to come to you if you'll just allow it.

Even though broadcasting was one of the smallest career fields (there were fewer than 300 of us in all ranks around the world), we had too many. So the Air Force instituted what they called a "drawdown." That meant if you wanted to get out early, you could. All you had to do was refuse your next set of orders to a new duty station.

As luck would have it, I soon received orders to go to Turkey.

Now on the one hand, I had always wanted to live in Turkey. On the other, I was in a long-term relationship, and I was in *love*, so I didn't want to leave Texas, where I was stationed. Because of the drawdown, I had the option to stay in Texas and apply for news anchor jobs to get a jump start on my civilian career. I could keep moving forward with no stagnation. It was awesome. The Air Force kindly gave me up to six months to get out of the military as part of the drawdown, and I could name my last day, or date of separation.

The smart choice would have been to pick a date six months out. That would have given me plenty of time to research jobs, network, send out resumes and anchor demo reels, and secure my next job.

But for some reason, I decided on two weeks. I literally cannot tell you what in the world I based that decision on. I guess I figured that premilitary, I was always able to find new jobs really fast and had always given two weeks' notice. I had no idea that most people search, on average, one month for every $10,000 they want to make in a year.

When I anchored my final newscast, I had a great goodbye party and left to start my job search from home. I had about three weeks of what the military calls "terminal leave," or saved-up vacation. Meanwhile, my then-fiancé and all of my friends were still in the service.

I wasn't prepared for what not being a part of the Air Force anymore would feel like. I don't think anyone can prepare you. It's probably different for everyone, but leaving the Air Force was *far harder* than leaving my family in Tennessee to go into the military. They had become my family. I've never experienced anything before or since that bonded me with people more.

It only took a couple of weeks of being at home searching for jobs to realize I had to find a way to occupy my time while searching for a position in television. I had cleaned our house from top to bottom, organized and alphabetized everything, then started doing projects. I started by cleaning the air ducts and then went on to having the tile restored. By that, I mean I was paying people to do the projects with money I should've saved until I had landed my next job.

I was going stir-crazy doing so little, so I went to my fallback solution of temporary agencies to earn some income and keep myself busy. But as there were no temp jobs for news anchors or reporters (which would have been awesome), I had to revert to my other in-demand skill set as an executive assistant.

That was hard for me. It felt like a big step backwards. I had that job in high school. And I had worked my tail off while I was in the Air Force to get a degree so I could move up the career ladder.

I also had bills to pay and a responsibility to contribute to the household. I've never been, nor will I ever be, too good for *any* honest work. Temp work would allow me to earn an income and continue to look for the job I wanted.

I chose to focus on the fact that an executive assistant role was always in demand and it paid well. That's not to say it didn't take a little convincing when I talked to the head of the agency. The role they were filling was to assist the vice president and the three directors of finance at a large company called Harland Clarke that printed paper checks for banks.

The head of the agency had never hired a veteran before and needed to be convinced that I could still type after seven years in the military, and that I understood spreadsheets and software. I had written my own scripts my whole career, so my typing was fine. My spreadsheet skills, however, were a little more lackluster than they looked on the test. Agencies test your skills on different software. I can, and did, score 100 percent on the tests, but here's the secret: that score means nothing more than I can navigate the software. Picture your grandma and her iPhone. Sure she can use it to call you and maybe even text you, but that's about it.

Nevertheless, I was hired!

The next challenge was wardrobe. Let me tell you, after nearly seven years of wearing a military uniform every workday and only having to choose my own clothes on the weekend, rushing into corporate life and buying the necessary clothing was daunting and expensive. I decided to raid T.J. Maxx and Marshalls, and only pick clothes that were either black or went with black, so I only needed one pair of shoes (black heels) and could make a work wardrobe out of as little as possible without anyone noticing.

My first day at Harland Clarke was exciting. I was thrilled to be back to work. Plus, it's always fun to learn and meet new people. Everyone was really nice and helpful. The only dark spot was that I was filling in for the current assistant because she'd experienced a tragedy in her family and needed time to deal with it. But I was glad I could help in some small way by making it easier for her to take the time and by ensuring her work was taken care of while she was gone.

In my first week, I met the CEO, Charles Korbell, in the elevator. I was honored, because everyone seemed to speak of him highly. While it might have made some people nervous to meet the person who ran the company, my years of interviewing high-level military leaders and officials had taught me that the folks in charge were often the nicest and the most down-to-earth.

As the elevator doors closed, he extended his hand. "Good morning, I don't think we've met. I'm Charles."

I shook his hand and smiled. "I'm April. It's a pleasure to meet you."

"What area are you in, April?"

"I'm down the hall in Finance for about three weeks, helping Ken's team."

"Ah, you're filling in for Elaine. I have her and her family in my thoughts and prayers." Before stepping out of the elevator, Charles turned to me. "Welcome, April. We're happy to have you here. If you need anything, just let me know."

"Thank you. I will!" I was impressed. He knew the name of an assistant and was concerned about her family. He had offered to help a temp. But he never once even alluded to the fact that he was the boss of everything.

I was also pleasantly surprised by how fun and exciting the people in Finance were. I've never particularly cared for math and thought people who wanted to base their whole career on it must be serious and quiet. But they weren't. They were great about getting work done, and I had a lot of fun helping them and learning from them.

Meanwhile, I was still doing phone interviews for television jobs. I quickly discovered that I'd likely need to move to get a job in broadcasting. My fiancé was open to moving as long as the salary was right and it was closer to his two young kids instead of farther away. Both conditions seemed very reasonable to me.

After a few interviews at different TV stations—and salary offers that made my former military paycheck look like a king's ransom—I began to wonder whether I should continue in broadcasting. I had loved it in the military, but I'd also done it for long enough to feel like doing something different could be a nice change.

Just a week later, I found out my fiancé's two little ones, ages five and three at the time, were coming to live with us. Meanwhile, he was still in the service and often traveled for a week or more at a time. I knew the change would already be a big one for them, and if I had a job that required me to work second shift while they were with a caregiver, it would be even harder for them. That just wasn't an option.

A lot of folks questioned why I was "giving up my dream" based on this new development, but I never felt like I gave anything up. I was ready for a new challenge. And I always felt strongly that if kids were in your life, you should give the best you have to offer. They deserved that, and I was honored to get to be part of their lives.

So with that change, I was now officially on the hunt for a job in business. I was really enjoying my time at Harland Clarke. By this point, I'd been with the company for two months. The assistant I was filling in for didn't return, and they hadn't found a replacement for her yet.

A few days later, as I was thinking about all the places where I should apply for a new job, I saw Charles in the elevator a second time.

I stepped in and smiled. "Hi! How are you?" I wasn't expecting him to remember me. I'd been a temp who was only supposed to be around for a few weeks, and he hadn't seen me for several months.

But Charles smiled back and said, "I'm great, April. I hear you are doing an amazing job in Finance and they'd love for you to stay."

I grinned and took a step backward. It was a large company with thousands of employees. I wasn't important in the grand scheme of things. However, Charles sure had a way of making me feel like I was.

"That means the world to me," I said. "Thank you. You made my day. I hope you have a great one too!" I waved as I stepped out, deciding then and there that I would stay. This was my kind of company. They cared about people, loved to hire veterans and lots of people already knew me, so it only made sense.

I applied for two marketing positions that were available online. I felt absolutely qualified.

Sure, I would have to learn certain skills, but I didn't think that would be hard or take too long. I was excited. If Finance was this fun, how fun would Marketing be! I waited for a phone call from Human Resources telling me that I had an interview time.

And I waited.

And waited.

Finally, I told Ken, the vice president of finance, I had applied for a job at Harland Clarke and hadn't ever heard back. He said he'd check on it for me, which I really appreciated.

I got a call from HR the next day. "Hi April, do you have a minute? I'm calling to offer you a role with us. Would you be interested?" I held the phone receiver away from my face and stared at it. That was fast! Without even an interview?

"Doesn't someone in Marketing need to talk to me first?"

"Um, no I don't think so. The role is in Finance."

My stomach sank. She meant the executive assistant role I already had.

She told me they wanted me full-time and were offering a salary $20,000 higher than the marketing positions I had applied for. That was a lot of money to me. However, even after just a few months, the job didn't interest me anymore. I'd improved on some processes and systems, and I was done with my work (taking care of four people) by noon every day. It just wasn't enough of a challenge.

I replied, "I thought you were calling about one of the two marketing positions I applied for. I'm not looking for a permanent role as an assistant, but thank you."

The HR rep said, "Okay. I think Ken will be disappointed, but I'll let the specialist hiring for the marketing jobs know that you aren't interested in this role."

I told Ken about the conversation and that I genuinely appreciated the offer, but that I wanted to do work that was more in line with my degree and offered a clearer path for growth within the company. He said he'd talk to the head of marketing for me. He also asked that I help interview new assistants to make sure he got a good one.

It was a deal!

The next week, the HR specialist in charge of hiring for the positions I wanted called me back. She said unfortunately I wasn't qualified for the roles because I didn't have the right skills. They wouldn't be forwarding my resume to Marketing for an interview. I asked if there were classes I could take or seminars that would help me learn what they thought I was missing.

She said, "No, I'm sorry. There's just too big of a gap between news anchor and marketing specialist."

She didn't sound sorry. She sounded irritated. And that struck me as odd. Isn't initiative a good thing? This business marketing specialist role didn't seem that complicated. I hadn't trained banks on how to order checks before, but surely it wasn't that hard to learn.

I had a great attitude, I worked hard, I could learn really fast—and I wrote checks all the time!

I thought maybe if she and her boss, an HR director, better understood the kind of person I was, they might reconsider. So I wrote them an email. (This was a benefit to already being inside the company I had decided needed to hire me.)

In my excitement, I didn't consult Ken on this decision. He was always giving me tips on how to strategize when talking to people. He taught me to pose my suggested improvements to other executives' work and reports with questions such as, "Do you think this would be more effective if you had two years' worth of data instead of just one?" instead of my more direct way of speaking, which was, "This report doesn't clarify what you're trying to say. It should have two years' worth of data."

Not being able to just tell people what was missing and how it could be better without worrying they'd be offended was one of the things I already missed about the military.

At least in my experience, people in the military always wanted to be and do better, and they didn't care if someone younger or less experienced had the suggestion that would help them do that. I was learning quickly that there were a lot more egos in corporate America, and people were much more likely to feel insulted instead of appreciative when you suggested improvements.

In my passion for the position, I may have forgotten that positioning strategy Ken often spoke of. Instead, I jumped right into the heart of the matter in my email.

To: Human Resources
From: April Shprintz
Date: February 22, 2005
Subject: Marketing Specialist Position Suggestions

Dear Sara,

I've been thinking about our discussion, and I really want to make sure that the right decision is being made for the company. I understand there are many skills for the Marketing Specialist Position that you don't feel I have based on my experience as a Television News Anchor, Executive Producer and Reporter, and my degree in Business Management.

I can imagine it is very difficult to hire the right person when you are looking for a specific list of skills. Since skills can easily be learned, I'd like to make a suggestion that worked very well for us in the military.

In situations where we had a position we needed to fill with a long list of qualifications that a great candidate didn't have, yet we knew the candidate would be perfect for the job, we submitted a revision for the job description so it better fit that candidate.

That may be exactly the solution we need here. You see, I didn't have any experience in broadcasting or a degree before I went into the Air Force. However, I was great at it! I was the top graduate of the Basic Broadcaster Course and the Advanced Electronic Journalism Course, and won countless Defense Media awards for my TV and radio work, including:

Number One Local Newscast
Best Local Television News Story
Best Local Radio Story
Outstanding Flagship Television Program
Broadcaster of the Year, AFN Europe
Broadcaster of the Year 1st Runner-Up AFHQ

This is only a few of the awards I won, and many of them were in my very first year of being a broadcaster. While I was learning, I also got the Air Force Outstanding Volunteer Service Medal for 1,000 volunteer hours with charities in one year! Imagine how much I could accomplish here if my singular work focus was being the best Marketing Specialist I can be.

I believe that people with great attitudes and work ethics who've shown high achievement in the past will be amazing at anything they do, and I would love to share that success with you in the Marketing Department.

As an added benefit, once you see how successful it is to rewrite a job description for the right candidate, you might want to add that to your hiring policy, so you don't miss out on any really great people.

I'm copying the Director of Human Resources on this email so she can see this idea too, as I think it will be very helpful for everyone in your department.

Looking forward to speaking with you soon!

April

I sent the email thinking surely they would conclude that I could go from brand-new to super-qualified fast, and was excited that I may have even helped them improve their entire process.

I followed up with voicemails to both of them letting them know I had emailed and was looking forward to speaking with them. Just in case HR didn't understand my plea, I sent a similar email to the head of marketing and left him a voice-mail about it as well. Then I awaited their replies and the offer of an interview.

Instead I got radio silence.

Reluctantly, I started applying to other places. It seemed like Harland Clarke just didn't want me if I didn't want to be an executive assistant. Still, Ken offered me that role a couple times a week. Each time, I smiled and said I knew his next assistant would be an even better fit.

For weeks, I wondered if maybe my email had gotten lost. I couldn't imagine they'd just ignored it.

And they hadn't. Apparently, my actions had become the stuff of lore in both Human Resources and Marketing. So much so that Don, one of the vice presidents who had owned and sold a very successful company of his own to Harland Clarke, called Ken to verify that this "Attila the Hun" everyone was talking about was really just a twenty-something-year-old girl who'd just gotten out of the service.

Ken told him that I was very bright, capable, and determined. He also said he would really appreciate it if someone would at least talk to me.

Don surprised him by saying he would interview me himself!

He was three levels above the marketing manager who was hiring for the role, but he loved the story. "I just want to meet her for myself," he told Ken. "She obviously doesn't take no for an answer, and I have a feeling she could be one hell of a salesperson."

That's what had led to this interview, during which Don had shared his concern about my tactics—and likened me to a barbarian warlord.

It was harder for me to read Don than anyone else I had ever met, and that included four-star generals during wartime. If I ever had to put together a poker team, he'd be my first call.

I worked diligently to keep my composure, even though I wanted to squirm under his gaze. I knew I could keep my cool. Thank you, military bearing and years under hot TV lights!

I confidently assured him I was up to the task.

Don nodded. "You're bright and polished, and you could do very well. We'd need to teach you more about communication and positioning, but you seem like a quick learner. I'll talk it over with the team, and someone will give you a call either way."

I walked back to Finance at the other end of the building having no idea how I had done.

"Well?" Ken asked.

I exhaled a huge breath. "I have no clue. Normally I can figure out people's impressions of me, but I couldn't read Don at all." I slumped down in my chair, exhausted.

Ken laughed. "Nobody can read Don. He's the best at asking questions and giving feedback while keeping his thoughts to himself. However, he doesn't usually interview anyone at the entry level, which could be a good sign…or he could've just been curious about you because you caused such a ruckus!" He chuckled again then added, "But I don't think that's it."

I took another big breath and decided that either way I wasn't going to feel bad about going after what I wanted with gusto. I understood that I had probably ruffled feathers, but I wasn't sorry about it. I simply didn't know how to go after anything halfway.

A couple days later, I received two job offers: one from another company and one from Harland Clarke for the business marketing specialist role, which I quickly accepted. I did it!

In my first five years at Harland Clarke, I was promoted four times, which allowed me to learn every aspect of the business. I was one of the company's top salespeople for many years.

Don took me under his wing and taught me more about strategy, positioning, and professional sales than anyone before or since. He put me in really hard positions and roles where clients were having huge problems (or downright hated us), and allowed me the autonomy to help them and to grow into truly trusting my business sense and instincts.

I saved several client relationships, earned the right to work with some of our biggest and best clients, helped them grow, and even completed a $90 million-plus sale before leaving to join a startup called nCino.

My role as a regional vice president at nCino led me to even more success, including my first seven-figure earning year and being a part of the sales team that helped build the company to a $7 billion valuation at its initial public offering, both of which were great experiences to prepare me for starting my own company, Driven Outcomes.

My Advice

Once again, I learned so much from this experience…and often from mistakes!

I hope you take away the knowledge that life absolutely isn't a race. Even if it were, we'd all be running completely different ones. The pace you run and the time you finish simply don't matter. What does matter is how much you enjoyed it along the way. I'm grateful I got to that way of thinking eventually, and I'd love it if you do so earlier than me.

Each experience I shared in this book gave me skills, knowledge, and confidence to eventually start my own company. At Driven Outcomes, I've dedicated my life to helping people make their impossible dreams possible. We do that together using the principles of The Generosity Culture, which I developed based on the example set for me by Aunt Sue.

Being generous with your time leads to the most amazing things. Companies that implement The Generosity Culture's principles of pouring into their people, their clients, and their community experience tremendous employee satisfaction, client loyalty, community impact, and financial success.

I help companies grow, scale, or turn around by believing in them and giving them the tools to realize their dreams. I also teach them how to nurture a belief in themselves.

Nothing is impossible. If we can dream it, it can become our reality. And the more people and companies that learn and demonstrate that, the better the world will be.

How does that apply to you? Simple. Even your wildest dreams aren't too wild. Your biggest goals aren't unrealistic. I'm not smarter, more talented, or more special than you, and all of my dreams have manifested, even against great odds. That means no matter what anyone else says—if you believe you can do it, you're right.

If you still need one other true believer to help you know it's possible, I'm right here.

And I'm rooting for you.

ABOUT THE AUTHOR

Photo by Mark Broadway Photography

April Shprintz has been described as a force of nature. She brings an infectious energy to both life and work, inspiring companies, CEOs, and leaders.

April's career has spanned the Air Force, corporate America, and her own firm—Driven Outcomes—where she works with companies globally. Her work has helped generate over $1 billion in additional revenue using the principles she created known as The Generosity Culture®. When April is not teaching companies how to "pour into" their people, their clients, and their community, she invests her time with various nonprofits helping children, veterans, and those experiencing homelessness.

April lives in Palm Beach Gardens, Florida, with her Shih Tzu, Cowboy, who serves as the Chief Dog Officer of Driven Outcomes and makes cameos in her video productions.

Made in the USA
Coppell, TX
10 October 2021

63835655R00081